Weaker Sections: Political Social Management in Indian Context

Edited by
Prof. Dr. Baldev Agja
Professor and Head
Post Graduate Department of Political Science
Sardar Patel University, Vallabh Vidyanagar

Publish World

2015

Weaker Sections: Political Social Management in Indian Context

Edited by
Prof. Dr. Baldev Agja
Professor and Head
Post Graduate Department of Political Science
Sardar Patel University, Vallabh Vidyanagar

Publish World

2015

Weaker Sections: Political Social Management in Indian Context

Copyright © Authors.

First Edition : 2015

ISBN : 978-81-928910-6-4

Published & Printed by
Publish World
Near Nandbhumi
A-V Road, Anand, Gujarat
http://www.publishworld.org
Email : pwisbn@gmail.com

Editorial Board

Prof. Kamlesh Dabhi
Associate Professor,
Department of Political Science
L.D. Arts College, Ahmedabad

Peer-Review Team **Dr. Dinesh S. Parmar**
Department of Political Science
Shree N.M. Shah Arts and Commerce
College, Shankheshwar, Dist: Patan.

Dr. Naresh Chauhan
Assistant Professor,
Department of Rural Economics
Gujarat Vidyapeeth, Ahmedabad
Project Director-ICSSR Sponsored
Research Project, SC Study, Gujarat

Dr. S.R. Bhaiya
Field Officer cum Head
Cost of Cultivation Scheme
Ministry of Agriculture, Govt. of India
Agro-Economic Research Centre,
Sardar Patel University, V.V. Nagar

Dr. Divya Patel
Assistant Professor
Shree J.M. Patel Arts College, Anand

Mr. Bharat Makwana
M.A., M.Phil (Political Science)

Mr. Anagat Vaghela
M.A., B.ed (Political Science)

Mrs. Chandrika J. Chavda
M.A., M.Phil. (Political Science)

Online Editors **Mr. Ankur Parmar,**
BA (English), Composer
Er. Siddharth Agaja
BE Computer

Forward

It gave me great pleasure chairing the Inaugural Function of One-day UGC-Sponsored International Conference on "Weaker Sections: Political Social Management in Indian Context" organized by the Department of Political Science of this University on 11 February 2015.

I had the pleasure of listening to the Inaugural Address delivered by the Chief Guest of the Function, Ms Bharulata Kamble from media organization based in UK; the Keynote Address delivered by Professor Ghanshyam Shah, National Fellow, ICSSR, New Delhi; the Guest of Honour, Professor Rohit Shukla, Retired Professor of Economics, Sardar Patel Institute of Economic and Social Research; and the special guest, Professor (Dr) Anand P Mavlankar, Professor of Political Science, M S University of Baroda, Vadodara.

I was happy to learn that many of the delegates would be presenting studied papers on issues that fall within the ambit of the Conference. The themes of the Conference seem to be interesting indeed and I felt that there would be adequate scope for discussion leading to some of the experts offering practical solutions to the problems faced by the weaker sections of our society. Such practical solutions would help our policy-makers frame good policies on these issues in future.

I am happy to learn that the department is now bringing out a collection of selected papers presented at the Conference in the form of a book. I congratulate the Department on their effort in this regard, and look forward to the impact that the book would make when it is published.

I wish the department good luck in its future endeavour!

Dr. Harish Padh
Vice-Chancellor
Sardar Patel University
Vallabh Vidhyanagar
Gujarat (India)

About Editor

Dr. Baldev Agja

Dr. Baldev Agja is a Professor and Head of the Post-graduate Department of Political Science, Sardar Patel University. He joined the University on 1994. He is also the Professor in-charge of Administrative Unit of Humanities & Social Sciences. He is a member of the Advisory Committee of the Indian Council of Social Science Research (ICSSR) state level studies on Educational Status of Scheduled Castes. He has also worked as a UGC nominee for the Planning and Monitoring Board of Kannur University, Kerala. He has worked in several other committees as co-ordinator. He is co-ordinating the UGC Sponsored NET Coaching Centre for SC/ST, Sardar Patel University. He is also rendering his services as the superintendent and Rector of two Hostels of Sardar Patel University. He has held academic positions such as Secretary in Gujarat Political Science Association, Hon. Director of Dr. Babasaheb Ambedkar Chair, Sardar Patel University, and an Executive Member of Indian Political Science Association. He has worked in a number of Sardar Patel University recognized academic committees and is appointed as a member in a number of UGC approved Expert Committees. He has served as Co-ordinator of Examination and Central Assessment Centre in all M.A. Exam, Humanities Building, Sardar Patel University. He has won the Best Research Article Award 2005 Sardar Patel Chair, Sardar Patel University.

Dr. Baldev Agja is a man of Research and is a recognized Ph.D. Guide in four universities of Gujarat state. 09 Research Scholars have successfully completed their doctoral research under his guidance. 02 International students are pursuing their research under his guidance. 10 students are reading for Ph.D. under his guidance at present. 09 scholars have been awarded the degree of M.Phil under his guidance.

He has offered services as the director of 13 state/national/international level seminars, conferences, orientation programmes. He has attended 399 seminars, conferences, symposia and has delivered Expert Guest Lectures in many seminars. He holds membership of many academic and professional bodies. He is associated with many NGOs. He has authored 10 Books and edited 02 books, and 52 articles. He is a member of Academic Review Committee and Advisory Board Member in four International Research Journals. Recently, he has successfully edited two books on weaker section of India.

Dr. Agja is serving on executive posts in various professional associations. He is an intellectual activist, social office-bearer and held various posts in various institutions. He also works for weaker sections' human rights.

Preface

Dr. Babasaheb Ambedkar gave a message – "Educates, agitates and organizes. "But what kind of education? Present education is fast becoming irrelevant to the changing needs. It is to be understood the present situation. Management refers to an activity of setting and achieving objectives. Management of human resources would help us to think on major issues affecting on weaker sections: political science management in Indian context. The predicament of the weaker section, which would be an outcome of such situations, is not in tune with the modern value of humanities. Political Science Post graduate department of Sardar Patel University always think about futuristic role of an individual in the context of management. Weaker section seems an individual part of India and the world. Person or people have to suffer which are in deprived section.

Rabindranath Tagore viewed education as a right which enables individuals and communities to act on reflection. Main aim of the conference is to think and act on weaker section of our country in the context of management. An individual man or society can be a bridge between the government and the society. At least one should know who is weaker? Why the weaker section has been established?

Article 39 certain principles of policy indicates us equality for all. And the policies lay down by government for weaker. Function of panchayati raj, situation of backward community, major issues of weaker can be discussed and steps should be taken by government and people for the upliftment of weaker. The condition of weaker in rural and urban area is not equal. There is major issue that the deprive people are not getting total help even though government has produced policies. Major issues like political empowerment of women through sources, impact of literature, condition of SC/ST and other minorities in the context of management, prevention of atrocity, welfare schemes for the weaker, strategies and programme for rural section are discussed by authors in present book. Discussion and concluding remarks are given in each paper of the issue which show us way to rethink on policies and political science management in the Indian context.

Today we need of more micro, small and rural entrepreneur. Management are attached with profit maximization, environment, socio- political issues, efficiency and equity. Today change in the policies, financial policies of government, taxation policies, policies of labour laws are needed to re-established.

Effective issues of weaker as a political science management in Indian context are discussed by the authors through the articles and papers in the present book. We wish to congratulate the entire author who gives opportunity to publish their articles/ papers through our journal. The issue of present journal will help us and think on remedial work for weaker. Researcher and student working in the field of education will be helpful to rethink on the present condition of deprive people in our country. We should think and act towards what remedies should be suggested for the betterment of the weaker.

Again I wish good luck and thanking to all for making the book qualitative by giving their valuable time and writing articles.

Prof. Dr. Baldev Agja
Professor and Head
Department of Political Science
Sardar Patel University
Vallabh Vidyanagar

Contents

Contents

WEAKER SECTIONS: POLITICAL SOCIAL MANAGEMENT IN INDIAN CONTEXT

Ghanshyam Shah
National Fellow, ICSSR, New Delhi

Political-Social Management is a subject matter of public management or public administration to improve condition of weaker sections of society. It is now euphemistically called governance. I therefore rephrase the subject as "Weaker sections and governance". At the outset, let me emphasize that governance should aim at empowering and enabling them to be equal citizens in democratic country and not recipients of dole, a charity. So that, they can live with dignity and enjoy equal say in decision making process to develop their potentialities to carve out their life chances.

Let me first of all identify weaker sections. These are the people who live in insecurity and struggle for survival. In general, agricultural laborers, forest laborers, small and marginal farmers, village artisans, casual laborers, self-employed –artisans, vendors etc. - in short all those who work in unorganized urban and rural sectors constitute economically weaker sections of society. They are poor and marginalized. They survive by selling their labor and/or minor product. They range from bonded laborers to supervisors, sells-persons. Their income vary from less than Rs.1500 to Rs.30, 000 per month. Social and economic insecurity haunt them. Besides economically deprived a large number of them are also socially and culturally oppressed and exploited by dominant classes.

Thanks to historical condition and nature of our social system in which primordial ties dominate, poor bania has more social and cultural capital than the poor belonging to fisherman community or Bareeya or Dalit caste. The formal has an edge over the latter in social and geographical neighborhood surrounding and social networks that influence life chances. In terms of caste and community majority of the weaker sections belong to scheduled castes (SC), scheduled tribes (ST), de-notified tribes (DNT), other backward castes (OBC), and religious minority communities, mainly Muslims. Over and above, women in general and of weaker sections in particular are most vulnerable.

These communities however are not homogeneous. They occupy different position in society and suffer from different kind of disadvantages. SCs occupy low social positions in caste hierarchy and have been deprived of certain opportunities to improve themselves. The SCs, also known as 'Anti-Sudras' or 'Dalits', suffer from the stigma of untouchability. The STs have different culture which has been looked down by the dominant social communities. For the last two centuries they are the victims of competing institutionalized religions which have cultural expansionistic agenda. Moreover, they have remained outside the mainstream of economic development, having their own economic and political system. OBCs though do not suffer from stigma like that of dalits, lack economic opportunities and exposure which hinder their path to avail new opportunities. De-notified tribes suffer from stigma as 'criminal', hence have limited access to modern economic avenues. In the nationalist discourse, Muslims are treated as 'others' anti-national, second class citizens. Women of all communities are the victim of patriarchy, and experience both caste/community as well gender discrimination.

These communities are economically and culturally stratified. A tiny section among them is economically well-placed though still not completely free from social discrimination. Among them one can get a handful number of families, except the Dalits, enjoyed political position at one time in the recent past. Because of a historical legacy, such individuals and their families have availed more economic opportunities than their brethren. Overall condition of these communities varies from region to region. For instance, condition of STs in central or east India is different than North–East India in several ways. Similar is

2

the case of several OBCs. In south India, particularly in Tamil Nadu some of the OBCs enjoy both economic and political power than Dalits of the region. Moreover, stratification within the communities has been sharpened in the last six decades. Vast majority continue to remain economically and educationally weak and deprived, but a tiny section has improved both in economic as well as political and socio-cultural spheres.

In this background, while evolving or evaluating governance in addressing the issue of empowering weaker sections four points need to be kept in mind. One, all communities undergo change, and their relationship with the dominant strata also change. Second, these communities are fragmented into several groups/jatis/communities competing with each other. Third, there is inter and intra stratification among these groups. Fourth, though all of them are economically deprived and victim of the larger economic system, they are also victim of different socio-cultural system, SCs are victim of caste system, tribals are victim of cultural as well as economic imperialism, Muslims and Christians are victim of majoritarinism, and women are victim of patriarchy. Therefore, a strategy and modus operandi to tackle the issue of weaker sections have to be addressed at two fronts simultaneously. One related to a larger economic system, and second concerned with socio-cultural systems.

Moreover, it needs to be underscored that political social management for emancipation of the weaker sections have to be a part of broader vision for society as a whole; and not in isolation. It is an issue of governance in totality, governance as a whole. I will now turn to governance.

Governance
It is truism and also tautological that the function of any government is to govern, manage socio-economic affairs of the country. Important is what kind of socio-economic relationship in society that the governance would prefer to maintain and/or attain? What are its long term and short term priorities? These questions are related to mission and

3

objective of the state for nature of socio-economic and political order to be developed. Theoretically the objective of the State is to govern society in a way so as to attain 'common good'. Common good is above private interests; convertible, or reducible, to the sum total of all the private interests of the individual members of society and interchangeable with them. It needs to encompass all the citizens and all aspects of happiness which include – economic, cultural, spiritual, social and political. In other words, normatively objective of the state in Buddhist philosophy has to be *Bahujan Sukhay, Bahujan Hitay (happiness and welfare of vast majority of the people)*. This is of course a lofty ideal which every state –modern or traditional, democratic or authoritarian would proclaim. But phases like happiness and welfare are vague. Happiness is subjective, and one can say that the poor is happy with her situation because she does not have many wants and ambition; and may believe in destiny. Welfare has an element of patronage and compassion on the part of the rulers. It does not necessarily believe in entitlement and rights of the citizens as equal. Therefore, this philosophy needs to be spelled out in modern context of democratic society in which an individual is a citizen and not a subject of the State.

In the modern world, objective of democratic state is, as enshrined in our Constitution; Liberty, Equality and Fraternity for all citizens. Equality includes social including gender and cultural which develops fraternity –brotherhood and sisterhood. And without equality, liberty as Dr. Ambedkar argued would be a liberty of a few powerful only. These three principles are interrelated. They go together. Inequality in substance hampers effective functioning of the political system and violates the liberty of those who survive at the lower layer of the social pyramid[1]. Greater inequality results in lesser possibilities for effective and meaningful participation of the deprived sections(s) in political

---

[1] Rawls (1971) defines the principle of justice for common good. The common good is the principle is the provision of compensating benefits for the least advantaged members of society.

processes. Their vulnerability in social, cultural and economic spheres provides them less space to be equal with those who are in upper echelons of the systems of production and reproduction. Strength of the powerful to manipulate choices of the vulnerable is related to the extent of gap between the two. Wider inequality hampers possibilities for the deprived to assert their voice. Therefore, the system of governance has to relentlessly build 'equal capabilities' for all its citizens particularly those who are deprived, oppressed and marginalized.[2]

In order to translate vision - of egalitarian social order embedded with freedom - in reality the state requires to develop an approach – a road map for economic development coupled with social inclusion. The state has to work out a mechanism and strategy for capital accumulation –map out available resources and also tap possibilities for new resources; and prioritize needs of a large section of society at a given point of time. This calls for formulating mega policy for capital accumulation through production system and distribution of the produced goods. Among others, there are two major perspectives for capital accumulation and distribution. One believes that the state facilitates capital accumulation by promoting and facilitating those who have capital. In the process, it is assumed that economic growth will percolate and will take care of distribution. There is another view which believes the intervention of the state is required both in the process of production as well as distribution. In the process of capital accumulation the state emphasizes on production system by prioritizing incremental needs of society. It monitors and regulates market/production mechanism. At the same time the States is engaged into

---

[2] It may be mentioned here that eradication of poverty does not necessarily generate egalitarian social order. Non-democratic political system –monarchy, benevolent dictatorship, oligarchy – also talk about eradication of poverty, partly out of compulsion to maintain social order and to prevent revolt, and also out of compassion. In democratic society eradication of poverty aims not only to provide basic necessities –food, clothing and shelter, but also to provide opportunities for development so that people become citizens and equal partners the system. (Shah 2010).

evolving as well as monitoring the process of distribution so as basic prerequisites needed for capacity building of all are met. The second view emphasis state intervention to build just egalitarian society. In India the architects of the Constitution debated this issue; though did not spell out the approach. While the Constituent Assembly was discussing the Preamble, Dr. Ambedkar asserted, "All of us are aware of the fact that rights are nothing unless remedies are provided whereby people can seek to obtain redress when rights are invaded...I do not understand how it could be possible for any future government which believes in doing justice socially, economically and politically, unless its economy is a socialist economy."

Vision for society is *sine qua non* for governance. Without vision centered around nature of economic growth, its sustainability, accumulation and distribution, social relationships among people, public morals etc, and wellbeing of all, in short perspective for desirable society governance is directionless and ad hoc. Vision is however not enough. In order to translate vision in the sphere of governance, the rulers have to comprehend the objective condition of society including availability as well as potentiality of resources as well as social milieu and location of societal power at a given point of time. On that basis the State needs to develop perspective and approach which get translated into policy measures. As mentioned above, there are different ways to move towards attaining 'desirable society'. As this conference focuses on role of politico-socio management for empowerment of weaker sections of society I assume that there is a consensus among us that state intervention is inevitable to perform this task. And, in the constitutional democratic system like India, it is expected that the government follows the approach within the objectives and premise of the Constitution.

Components of Governance

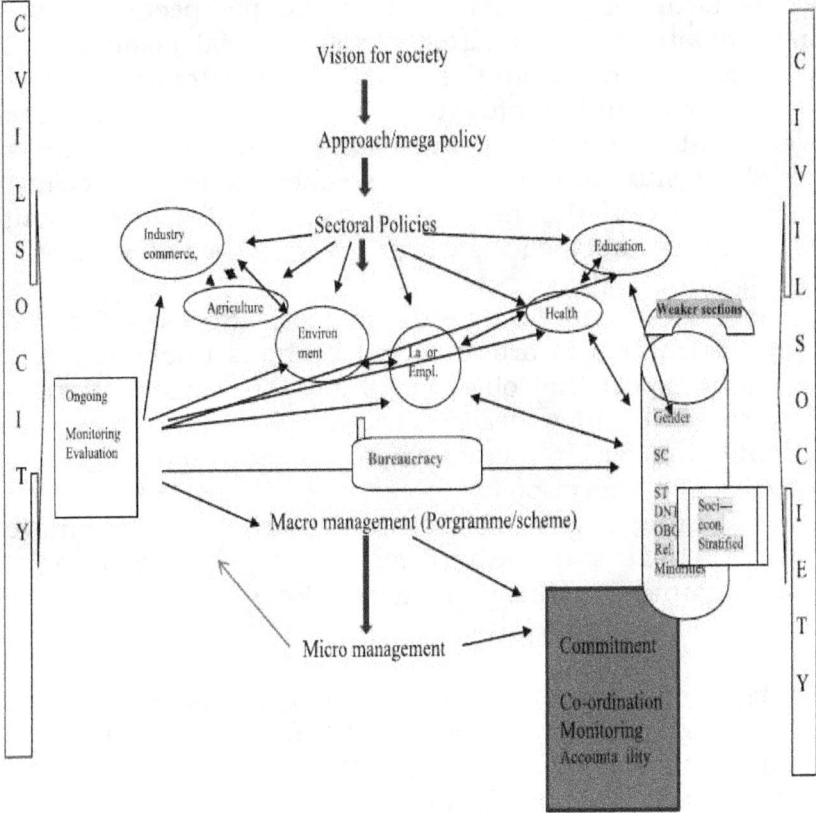

CIVIL SOCIETY (left margin)

Vision for society

↓

Approach/mega policy

↓

Sectoral Policies

- Industry commerce,
- Agriculture
- Environment
- La or Empl.
- Health
- Education.
- Weaker sections
  - Gender
  - SC
  - ST
  - DN
  - OBC
  - Rel. Minorities
  - Soci—econ. Stratified

Ongoing Monitoring Evaluation

Bureaucracy

Macro management (Porgramme/scheme)

↓

Micro management

Commitment

Co-ordination
Monitoring
Accounts ility

CIVIL SOCIETY (right margin)

Overall and Sectoral policy

Management follows from policy. The state formulates overall policy postulates, based on its comprehension regarding prevailing objective situation. Of course reading and interpretation of the objective situation depends upon one's perspective and concern. Reading of societal situation is different from the perspective of the dominant stratum that already enjoys social position and power than the one from the weaker sections of society who are exploited and subjugated. In such a situation, the government which is concerned for equality of all requires to read the situation from below, weaker sections of society. On the basis of the reading and vision the government policies formulates policies which involves the following.

1. Short term and long term policies: Process of social transformation is arduous and perhaps unending. One cannot expect that objective of equality can be attained overnight or in a decade. In the given resources and conflicting power relationships, the government has to evolve short term policy to carry out the objective which meets immediate needs and builds possibilities to move to the next stage. Short term objective needs to be transitional leading to meet long term objective incorporated in the vision.

2. Integrated sectoral policies: keeping the large policy in consideration, Government formulates from time to time policies for different sectors such as industry, agriculture, labour, health, education, infrastructure, urban-rural development, Women/SCs/STs/DNTs /OBCs/minorities' welfare etc. Legislations and then laws and by laws, rules and procedures follow. For sustainable development and smooth and good/balance governance sectoral policies as well as laws need to be mutually complementary to attain a large goal. For instance industrial policy need to be complimentary with agriculture and have to be labour intensive in a country like ours that provide decent employment. So is education and health policy. If sectoral policies are not integrated and move in different directions, overall

8

objective for egalitarian social order get ruptured and generate tensions and contradictions.

3. Trade-off: Objective situation is not always neat and clean for making sectoral policies. It often faces dilemmas between priorities. Given the situation the state requires to prioritize one over another at a given time. The choice is often difficult. For instance, a small section of the deprived communities has higher education but unable to compete with others for variety of reasons including bias as well as so-called lower level of merit and efficiency. In such a situation a tradeoff is between so-called merit and preferential treatment to the members of the deprived communities. Indian state has decided for the latter with a proviso that it cannot be the permanent solution for egalitarian social order.

4. Simultaneous priority: In the trade off situation priority to one over another is a temporary strategy of governance to meet immediate needs. At the same time state needs to address the other aspects also. And process has to be built up to deal with both the aspects simultaneously. For that, along with giving preferential treatment the state needs to evolve mechanism so that biases and discrimination from the system get weakened and eventually eliminated. Simultaneously, the state has to invest in building the capacity of the members of the deprived communities so as eventually provisions for the preferential system need not require. This calls for a system to provide universal quality education and skill development to all at every level. For that private education system which generates, perpetuates and strengthens inequality in society has to be banned. This has to be a foundation for employment as well as providing orientation to the students to intermingle with each other in the same milieu so as they imbibe values for equality and justice, develop fraternity and overcome cultural biases.

5. No retrograding measures: Most important consideration for the empowerment of weaker sections

should be to keep away from any retrograding policy that adversely affect condition of the have-nots leading to further pauperization by taking away their resources and displacing them.

6. Feedback, Monitoring and evaluation: Monitoring and evaluation have to be inbuilt in all the programmes. With their evidence based feedback, the programs and even policies need to be modified.

In order to translate various policies of different sectors and target groups such as weaker sections the government formulates various programs/schemes for implements. The programs to empower weaker sections may be of three categories: (1) Exigent, (2) Transitional (3) Equalizing and universal. The exigent programs should focus on basic needs such as food security, potable water and primary health care services. The schemes for BPL families such as widow pension, old age pension, for disabled persons etc. require to be carried out on war footing. The transitional programs include subsidies to small and marginal farmers, artisans and also providing preferential opportunity for employment and higher education to deprived communities. The equalizing and universal programs include education, health care, skill development and decent employment with social security to all.

Next step is implementation of policy through macro (state) and micro-level management. Management – organizational structure, rules, procedures, line of command, co-ordination, delegation of power, etc. – to implement programs meant for empowering weaker sections has to be poor people friendly. The organization (s) responsible for implantation has to be decentralized and should make all efforts to identify the people and households entitled to get benefit of the schemes. It should not be other way round that the people are required to go to offices with proofs and experience humiliation. And more important the government should approach the poor people not as recipients of charity or patronage but as entitled citizens.

The rules and procedures of these programs have to be less complicated, more transparent and participatory with a built-in accountability. Power and responsibility both at the micro and macro level, horizontally as well as vertically need to be well defined and identified. Co-ordination among the various divisions/wings need to be maintained. Supervision and regular monitoring of the targets makes the governance effective. The organizational structure need to be built up with rewards and punishment to the persons responsible for implementation.

In this process bureaucracy plays a central role. After six decades of Independence ethos of bureaucratic structure continues to be of the British days, indifferent to common person. Caste and class character of bureaucracy on the whole is not sympathetic to the everyday problems of the marginal sections of society. While implementing these programs the bureaucracy has to be oriented in the egalitarian vision of society. Intensive and repetitive efforts have to be made to change their mindset of Brahminical value system embedded with what Dr. Ambedkar called 'graded- inequality'. They have to be geared to be pro-poor people. They need to be encouraged to be imaginative, flexible in procedures and rules. They need to create an environment giving confidence to illiterate poor that s/he can directly express difficulties and get help. Bureaucrats involved in pro-poor welfare programmes need to be oriented to empower poor as a citizen. At the same time accountability and transparency of the bureaucrats as well as elective representatives need to be inbuilt in administrative mechanism.

In short political-social management for empowering the weaker sections should be embedded with the principles of liberty, equality and fraternity to build egalitarian society.

WEAKER SECTIONS AND SOCIO-POLITICAL MANAGEMENT

Rohit Shukla

Prof. of Economics (Retd.), Sardar Patel Institute of Economic and Social Research, Thaltej Road, Ahmedabad.

1. Introduction

Beginning from the last quarter of the last century, the world has witnessed revolution in digital technology. This revolution has changed many old equations, patterns and styles. Many ideas and ideals which were considered either "given" or were accepted as "time tested" are now considered tangential or irrelevant. Social and Political Ethics is one such area. While the digital technology has helped in such directional change, many other factors like demographic pressures, environmental crisis, Globalisation and neo-liberal approach and above all, crony capitalism has placed very heavy demands on the style , objectives, and content of government functioning. This has inevitably given rise to many contradictions and conflicts. While in case of India, globalisation has been operating under the circumstantial existence of neo-liberalism in case of China it is globalisation sans neo-liberalism. However, in both cases, crony aspect of capitalism is persistent. In essence this underscores the significance of so called *"development"*, which is conveniently defied by the corporate world and defended by the political system. The political system craves for continuation of power and the corporate world aims at (unlimted) maximisation of profit. Such mix of power and profit drives the crony capitalism of the modern world order. Anything not in tune with such development is blasphemous.

This situation creates a space in which, issues of management of social and political aspects of a given society attain a central stage. It also becomes an area in which objectives, ethics and style of governance play very significant role. Thus, issues of management and governance in the overall context of development and social justice are always in a state of flux . It appears that these issues keep on constantly redefining themselves. In the context of Joseph Schumpeter (1942) there is a process of "creative destruction." In case of states like Gujarat, where the issues of so called "development" are raised to a very high pitch, a special focus is required in order to understand the mix of management and governance from the angle of social justice and crony capitalism. This becomes an interesting area of inquiry into socio-political management also.

2. Management: Some Issues

Management refers to an activity of setting and achieving objectives. Management includes a number of activities. There could be marketing management. There also could be management of human resources or natural resources. Managing production, choosing appropriate technology, minimising cost and maximising profits are also important issues in management. Along with land labour and capital management is a *resource* and is considered a factor of production. As such it is also concerned with creating appropriate corporate policies such that the firm/unit of production earns highest possible profit.

In this context, a manager or a team of management is hardly required to take a look at issues related with social justice. In the globalised world it is required to give highest importance to efficiency in resource use. Ideally speaking, such efforts are good for the economy as well as the society. However, in most of the cases, profit maximisation is not the end result but the main objective of the corporate policy. Implicitly and more so with crony capitalism, the aim is that of minimising costs and for this reason the corporations devise policies that will minimise all cost like those of wages, rent and interest.

2.1 Profit Maximisation and Management

Usually corporate management is viewed as a process or system in which the stated objective is that of profit maximisation. A firm is aiming at working for the

13

benefits of the share holders. For this purpose it is aiming at adopting any means such that the interests of the share holders are promoted to the maximum possible limit. In such a situation a firm, which is dealing with risks of various types and competitions from other firms has to plan for actions which will ensure a situation of minimum risk and uncertainty.

2.2 Socio-Political Management

The workings of corporations also calls for a management stance in which corporate houses have to influence the state policies in a large number of fields-both economic and socio-political. Government policies regarding taxation control and regulations of various types as well as trade commerce and environment affect the competitive character of a big corporation. In fact the bigger the corporation larger is the size of risk and the areas from which such risk arise also is very large.

2.3 Globalisation, MNCs and Management

Management is the buzz word in the field of MNCs. The field of management has been constantly expanding. It is no more related to economics and finance or marketing. With globalising world, management too is called upon to perform a variety of tasks. Socio-political management is one such area. As the size of an MNC expands, its exposure to various types of risks also increases. Such risks may arise out of change in the ruling party, change in the leadership of a party, change in the tax and industrial policies, changes in the structural constituents of an economy and so on. The risk factor is also affected by societal phenomena like traditions, food habits, and migration and so on.

2.4 State and Management in the context of Neo-Liberalism

State is a powerful mechanism, which can deliver welfare for the people if it so desires. However, under the neo-liberal philosophy a minimalist role for the state is assumed. Under this situation, welfare is not a matter of any direct action or a stated policy of a state. It is presumed that the market is competent enough to deal with both welfare as well as growth aspects of the economy. There is a faith in the theory of trickle down or percolation and the benefits of growth are assumed to percolate down and as such no market interventionist policy framework is needed.

In this situation, since the corporate world is the main hero of the act, state is required to set policies which are conducive to faster growth. 'Roll the red carpet' for the MNCs as well as industry in general so that the economy is ambient about investment. Even the issues of environment and pollution or for that matter even regarding labour laws are sometimes considered to be hindrances to the growthmanship.

2.5 CSR and Management

CSR or corporate social responsibility is considered to be a sort of social welfare oriented responsibility of the corporate world. It is a known fact that in recent years in the U.S. , persons like Bill Gates and Warren Buffet have donated huge sums from their personal properties for some good social cause. Earlier examples of Ford Foundation, Rockefeller Foundation, etc. are also time tested. Some Indian corporate houses like Wipro and Infosys are also known for their work for the upliftment of weaker sections of the society. However work of many corporations has been criticised for various reasons.

It is being increasing criticised that the CSR is not a purely welfare work. Some believe that it is part ethical and part business acumen. The argument is that the corporate houses try to remove conflict situations which may arise because of their operations leading to profit maximisation.

2.6 Management and Environment

The corporate world is also found to indulge in internalising environmental resources. In case of China, natural resources like air, water, and land are so much internalised that there are days when the citizens are advised to stay indoors lest they are suffocated by the thick and poisonous smog engulfing large urban areas.

2.7 Competition or Connivance?

In the history of American capitalism, era of 'Anti-Trust movement' is well known. Corporations formed and forged monopolies so that the risk of competition could be either minimised or entirely done away with. Thanks to the proactive state the anti-trust acts became effective. In developing countries of these days, either due to apathy of the civic society or due to media propaganda, crony capitalism persists and propagates.

2.8 Efficiency and Equity

Neo-Liberalism rests its credentials as a profound discourse on efficiency. In its theoretical build-up, it talks of unique advantages accruing to the society due to competition and efficiency. However, it is observed that inequality is high and also on the rise. Since the days of "Housing Bubble" in the U.S. , there are many serious dissents, which are expressed occasionally by various civic society groups. If Housing bubble arose in the year 2008, the reactions were felt in the years, 2010 onwards. First the Paris Riots of 2010 , where more than 10,000 cars were damaged or vandalised by youths.; this was followed by "Occupy Wall Street" demonstrations and "London Riots" of 2011. This period also saw the rise of "Arab Spring" originating fist in Tunisia.

Due to market failures and the resultant business cycles, phenomena of people versus State were rampant. In certain cases it was due to failure of the education system. Under the new policy of free market, education not only became extremely expensive but also became a cause for increasing inequality. Access to education was denied to all those who could not afford the high price of it. In the prevailing Indian context, parents were forced to choose between the education of a daughter and son. Since their household budget did not permit the cost of education for both the children. Thus the high price of education has resulted in increasing the gender gap in education, which, otherwise also, was high due to social system of discrimination. This discrimination was reinforced by market phenomenon of high price of education. One wonders about the role of the state in such a situation.

3. Weaker Sections : Some Broad Characteristics

Weaker sections could be identified as those belonging to three main groups:

(a) Vulnerable groups: People working in rainfed agriculture often face droughts and scarcity situations. They tend to lose a significant proportion of their output. Over the years, their capacity to survive on traditional ways of agriculture is eroded by frequent droughts and usurious practices of money lending. Whatever might be their initial conditions over the years they become weak. This process tends to add to the inequality prevailing in the economy.

(b) Socio-politico-religious aspects: There is a whole mix of reasons that characterise the weakness of certain specific groups of people. Women are traditionally weak. Besides, dalits, tribals and those living in remote areas are also weak compared to their counter parts placed differently. Culture and traditions along with religious beliefs and identities play an important part in this build up.

(c) Occupations and professions: Workers in the unorganised sectors provide an example of this type. Thus those working in Bidi or Agarbatti making , salt pan workers etc. are found to be weak. One of the reasons for this lies in the changing structure of market demand for the   products   which   are   produced   by   certain professions.Hand loom and Khadi workers and those who belong to handicrafts making also fall under this category. Economic weakness goes well with other kinds of weaknesses like political, social, cultural etc. These groups are not sufficiently empowered to influence their own earnings   in the markets. In a traditional society   even certain trades and professions are not open for all its members. Scavenging, taking off the hides of the dead animals and disposing of their carcasses etc., are not only low paying but its operators suffer from various stigmas as well. Their capacity to bargain for proper payments for their work is next to nil.

3.1 EWS: The Government Reckoning

According to the present government reckoning, the income limit for calibrating the weaker sections from others is likely to be raised from the present level of Rs. 3,300 /- to Rs. 6,000 /- a month. Practical implication of this lies in the process of urbanisation. Because of the rapid industrialisation large number of rural households will be required to migrate to urban centres. In order to provide cheap loans to them the Government thinks that the total urban poor may be a large chunk of nearly 81 million persons out of a total of 286 million urban dwellers. It is also expected that the number of EWS may rise by almost 40 percent in the near future.

However, housing and that to urban housing is not the lone area asking for support for the weaker sections. Nutrition and health care too are areas in which large scale efforts are required. If one has to believe Dr. Binayak Sen, the well-known human rights defender, the situation is really alarming. His data reveal the following:

- Thirty-seven per cent of India's adult population,
- 50 percent of the scheduled caste (SC) population and
- 60 percent of the scheduled tribe (ST) population suffer from chronic under nutrition.

3.2 Economic Growth and the Weaker Sections

A sharp mismatch between economic growth and human development is brought by the HDI. If one considers various HDRs of the UNDP one finds some clear observations to support this point; some of which may now be briefly mentioned.

- India finds a place in the top 10 fastest growing economies in the world.
- Its HDI rank is 119th in a total of 169 nations.
- This disparity in two areas of performance is due to high level of economic inequality.
- India ranks behind even some of the developing countries like Russia (69th rank), Brazil (73rd), China (89th).

- The Multidimensional Poverty Index identifies serious simultaneous deprivations in areas such as health, education and income. The country ranks 122 among 138 countries. It also shows that around 55 percent of Indians are poor.Of the total poor, a majority of whom live in rural India, 47 percent are tribals. Further, eight Indian states are home to 421 million multidimensionally poor people. This is more than the figure of 410 million in 26 poorest African countries. The states include Bihar, Madhya Pradesh, Rajasthan and Uttar Pradesh, often referred to as the BIMARU states.
- On the Gender Inequality Index, India is ranked 122nd out of 138 countries, based on 2008 data. The report says 27 percent of adult women in India have a secondary or higher level of education, compared with 50 percent of men. It is also to be noted that for every 100,000 live births, 450 women in India die from pregnancy-related causes, while the adolescent fertility rate is 68 births per 1,000 live births. Female participation in the labour market in India is 36 percent, compared with 85 percent for men.

4. The Daewoo Case

Amjad Hajikhani, Pervez Ghauri and Joon-Woo Lee of the Dept. of Bissiness studies , Uppsala University ,Sweden; School of Business Administration Manchester University and Inje University Korea have studied the Korean Motor Car Company Daewoo in the context of its operations in Poland. They offer a theoretical observation:

"The competitive strength of an MNC in international markets is defined by its behaviour in two different market arenas; the business and the socio-political. While international and industrial marketing studies, specifically in business network, have extensively explored relationships between firms, they rarely touch upon the socio-political relationships....The view of a social-cultural market positioning basically divides the entire business activity into two different but interwoven market arenas; one is the business competitive position, which considers the interaction with business actors, and the other, the

19

socio-political competitive position which concerns the interaction not only with social-political actors, cultural and aid organizations but also with business actors. The outcome in the latter situation subsidizes the first one. Creation of influence by interaction with socio-political and other non-business actors is attractive to MNCs for several reasons. It strengthens the competitive position of the firms as it reduces the cultural distance and the organizational or marketing costs. A lack of competence to provide a unique solution makes the actions of the 25 socio-political actors coercive and weakens the firms' business competitive position in the market.(P. 40)

"The case illustrates that the more progress a firm has made in its internationalization of business activities, the more advanced is its socio-political commitment."(P.35) The wider context of MNCs and Globalisation along with socio-political management thus becomes significant in influencing a wider area of existence and identity. Some of the issues can be broadly mentioned :

- Since economic rationality of profit maximization involves risk aversion as well as risk management, the socio-political field cannot be left out from the purview of corporate management. Thus involvement in the political structure and processes becomes imperative for the management of an MNC.
- In a given situation, for a developing country, there would be a number of MNCs competing for space for profit maximization. A successful MNC has to influence the state policy such that the competitors are kept in a disadvantageous position. Though this could be considered a part of the economic rationality paradigm, it is far removed from the arguments developed in favour of globalisation and neo-liberalism. Neo-liberalism pins its favourableness over other discourses on the ground that it will provide a competitive atmosphere such that economic resources will be harnessed with efficiency. Efficient and optimum resource use caused by open and free completion is the spirit of neo-liberalism. By indulging in socio-political

management this very foundation is challenged. This is an inherent contradiction of the system.

- The MNCs have to plan their socio-political management such that it has a more or less insulated area of operations. There is little competition and little risk of any type. the risk factors could emerge from any or many of the following:
  o Change in the industrial, export-import, or such other Government policy mix.
  o Change in the taxation policy
  o change in the financial policies including those related with interest rates and inflation
  o change in the policy or system of resource pricing and allocation.
  o change in the labour laws

The MNCs can bring in large chunks of FDI when the entire atmosphere becomes favourable to them. Naturally, this is bound to have many far reaching implications for the society-its political system, economy as well as its socio-cultural structures.

5. Weaker –Sections and Empowerment :: Present day concerns:

The predicament of the weaker sections , which would be an outcome of such situations is not in tune with the modern values of humanity. It violates human dignity and forces an economic rationale for inhuman acts like those of child labour and bonded labour. It also subjects them to a life full of avoidable miseries like those arising from mal-nutrition, unhygienic living conditions , lack of proper education, etc.

On the other hand, empowerment of the weaker sections cannot be achieved only by the state. In particular, a state which is notorious for issues like corruption can hardly be called upon to deliver in this situation. Thus it has to be dealt with in the overall realm of social action and awareness.

We live in an age in which companies equivalent in wealth of countries call the shots and control much of the earth's resources. Because corporates intervene in so many areas of social life, they must be responsible towards society and the environment. In India as well as in the rest of the world there is a growing realisation that capital markets and corporations must be made to serve the society as well. They also have some responsibility towards weaker sections of the society and not only towards the shareholders. And that consumers and citizens' campaigns can make all the difference in this scenario. For example, in the U.S. students have boycotted products of the companies which are not environment friendly.

In the age of globalisation, corporations and business enterprises are no longer confined to the traditional boundaries of the nation-state. One of the key characteristics of globalisation is the spread of the market and the change in the mode of production. The centralised mode of production has given way to a highly decentralised mode of production spread across the world.

References
1. Joseph Schumpeter (1942), 'Capitalism, Socialism and Democracy', Harper, New York.
2. http://www.globalcompact.org
3. The Economic Times, November 8, 2010
4. The Hindu, November 5, 2010
5. The Hindu, May 25, 2011
6. The Statesman, May 24, 2011
7. http://www.hindustantimes.com, November 2010
8. http://www.livemint.com, November 2010
9. http://sify.com, November 2010
10. "The Socio-Political Behaviour of Multinational Corporations in the context of Business Networks-The case study of the Korean MNC in a European Country," Amjad Hadjikhani, Pervez Ghauri and Joong-Woo Lee, Department of Business Studies, Uppsala University, School of Business Administration, Nancheter University and Inje University, Korea.

UNTOUCHABILITY AS LIVED SOCIAL EXPERIENCE: QUESTIONING PEACE IN VILLAGES

Dr. Prem Anand Mishra
Assistant Professor, Peace Research Centre
Gujarat Vidyapith, Ahmedabad

Abstract

The article intends to present untouchability as lived social experiences based on the first-hand experience of the researcher gathered in some of the Gujarat's and Bihar's villages. Employing 'experience as framework', it is argued here that untouchability expresses itself in various different new forms even today where so-called forward castes have discovered certain 'new ways' to keep themselves 'protected and purified' against the so-called untouchables. Such recent personal 'protective behaviour' of the forward castes towards the untouchables cannot be challenged legally as they do not come under the legal ambit. Yet they show how, at least in the some of the Gujarat's and Bihar's villages where the study was carried out, there was a silent and non-negotiable boundary between the forward castes and untouchables. Strikingly, this boundary is accepted by both so-called forward castes and untouchables in the villages and they do not try to cross it. Thus, one may find a 'peaceful condition' in the villages from outside. However, one may observe and analyze that how these villages show a kind of structural and cultural violence where perceived peace is divided into pieces. This further puts a big question mark on the limits of legal remedy of untouchability, on the other hand compels us to recall Gandhi's idea and practice of removal of untouchability through a radical social transformation based on 'change of mind', 'change of heart' and 'change of situation'.

Introduction and Argument

Untouchability is major complex social problem in India and it is in practice since ancient times in different form. It is a form of discrimination which is based upon caste which is pervasive in nature. For thousands of years, the practice of untouchability has marginalized, terrorized and relegated a section of Indian society to a life that is marked by violence, humiliation and indignity. Thus, untouchability is a form of both structural and cultural violence. It is cultural violence as it is sanctioned by the dominant religions of India, Hinduism, in its most vocal form while all other major religions in India participate in the perpetuation of untouchability. Moreover it is lived experience of all people in India – as a survivors or challengers. There are approximately 164.8 million *Dalits* are in India which are victims of untouchability (Michael 1999, 25). After Independence, Indian Constitution abolished and prohibited the practice of untouchability, yet it is in practice even today. There is no doubt that today the practice of untouchability is not as visible as it was in past but it does not mean that it has completely disappeared (Shah 2006: 73). In this regard, there is a general argument that modernization and after 1991 in the regime of Liberalization, Privatization and Globalization (LPG), untouchability is disappearing from Indian society both in villages and cities. This kind of argument is based on the assumption that LPG would increase inter-dependence and barrier between castes would disappear. This study suggests that in modern time interdependence among different castes are increasing but untouchability is not disappearing. In fact, it is taking new forms to perpetuate it. Thus, the paper argues that modernization and globalization have not resolved the discrimination between so called untouchables and *Savarna* or forward castes. It has just shifted the relationship between them because of compulsive economic interdependence.

Research Setting: Experience as Framework

The paper is based on the field experiences of the researcher carried out in some of the Gujarat villages, during Gramjivan Yatra (since 2008 to 2014 every year organized by Gujarat Vidyapith, Ahmedabad close to Gandhi Jaynati, 2 October). The findings of these experiences are collaborated with the researcher's experience of the two villages of Bihar- Mow and Sherpur- also. These experiences might be seen as lived experience of changing form of untouchability in 21st Century.

Experiences from Gujarat villages

Kanpara is village situated near Than, Chotila. In 2009, the researcher found that most of forward caste teachers in primary schools in this village using their own glass for their water. When asked, they argued that they do it because of 'health reason'. However, when discussed deeply they confessed that it is because that most of students are from lower caste thus they cannot get water from them or with the common glass. This phenomenon was seen in other villages as in Mangrol (Banaskatha 2012), Palaj, Ahmedabad (2008), and in Jesda (2013). In Palaj, there was another shift of untouchability observed in which it was noticed that a particular forward class family does not send their children to other village boys as others were untouchables. When the parents were asked they told that these untouchables speak rough language and their children will also learn that thus it is better to keep them in home. Interestingly children of this particular family are given freedom to watch TV and play computers games to spend evening. In morning these children go to Ahmedabad school in Van and come back by the evening. It shows how modern means are used to create separate space for children and how they remain totally cutoff from the village. There is recent phenomenon of temple building by almost all castes in some of the villages. In Mangrole (2012), it was also noticed that there were five temples in the villages and four were under construction. These under construction temples were of lower castes. These temples have become the symbol of caste identity and matter of status for castes. What is important to note that this phenomenon seems suggesting the affluence of some castes including the untouchables, however at the same time it also shows the isolation in villages. In other words, villages have become rich but untouchability still exists in different forms.

Cases from Bihar

If some of Gujarat villages show untouchability in different forms, Bihar the poorest state of India show the same phenomenon. In the study of two villages of Bihar - *Mow* and *Sherpur*, it was found that although there is economic interdependence between different castes - lower and higher including untouchables but when the tradition and ritual come, people of higher caste observe untouchability in some very sophisticated forms.

The most striking case is recent phenomenon of inter-dinning (*bhoj*) in the villages of Bihar. Traditionally forward caste did not allow untouchables to dine with them on the occasion of *bhoj* organized in *marriage, Janau and shradha*. Now under the compulsion of interdependence of different castes because of economic reason, upper caste people allow lower caste people to dine but in a very different way. Usually on the particular day of *bhoj* (Marrige, *Janau or shradh,* according to rituals) only same caste or community people are allowed to have dine together and that food are called *Kachha khana* (prepared by women of the same caste family). This *bhoj* is organized in the premises of the house of the organizer of the *bhoj*. For the other caste people, the higher caste family organizes another *bhoj* on second day of real *bhoj*. This *bhoj* for other caste is organized at very distance from the house of bhoj organizer and food is prepared by professional cook called *Halwaai*. Here food served is called *pakka Khana*. It is quite surprising to note that this second bhoj is quite lavish and has its own charm. It is important to note that 'serving' is also altered in second bhoj. While in *'real bhoj'* same caste people serve their caste community, in second *bhoj* only Other Backward Castes (OBC) Class people serve the all people. Here they work as intermediates. In marriage generally forward caste people arrange a separate vehicle for other caste people. These 'other' do not go in *Barati* with forward caste people nor do they take part in other marriage related rituals. They reach at marriage place in arranged vehicle and get food in isolated way and back very soon from the venue. In this way they become part of the marriage at the same time they remain untouchable.

26

It is also important to note that in recent time, this tradition of 'separation but show of interconnectedness' is also being repeated by so called lower class. When lower class organizes some events on the occasion of marriage, or death of someone, they also invite forward class people to join. Here the lower class people make good arrangements for dinning for higher class people and food is prepared by *Halwaai*, and forward class people have no objection in that as it is permitted to take food prepared by *Halwaai*. Here again food is served by some OBC Class people and forward class people have no objection in that. In one of the incident in which the researcher was also present, it was found that a *Dusadh* (untouchable community of Bihar) family arranged a *bhoj* on the marriage of his brother and many forward class people joined it. Initially the chief of that *Dusadh* family greeted all of forward class people but quickly on the pretension of some other work left the *bhoj* place and everything was in the hand of some OBC People and forward class people. It shows how untouchability is accepted by both higher caste and lower caste and a middle path are being made to preserve the economic interrelatedness.

Conclusion

These experiences show two important things. First, because of atrocity act higher caste people do not practice untouchability openly, but at personal level they are doing it in different form as seen above from using separate glass to not sending their children to play with other lower caste children. This tells us that village is still more a kind of collection of caste 'cell'. Each caste cell has confined itself to its fix boundary and they do not try to intrude other caste. Because of modern means of transportation and other entertainment facilities people of different caste do meet but at very core level they feel separate from each other. Physical distance may seem disappearing but mental distance among different castes still exists. Because of law against untouchability and other policies, forward caste people also feel that government is with untouchables thus they do not help their close other caste people and leave them to the mercy of the government. Untouchables and

27

other caste people when get affluence, they seem to assert their identity by making temples of their respective god or goddess.

Because of modernity and LPG, economic interconnectedness among different castes has increased. It has created a new tension in the village as people who live together now also work together. But long tradition of cast barrier and untouchability put a big question to be resolved in their lives. As seen in the above cases, this question has been resolved by employing OBC as intermediate classes between higher and lower classes. This shows a new shift in the practice of untouchability.

Finally village that seems peaceful from outside is divided into pieces even today. Here one may recall Gandhi's idea of change of heart and mind of forward classes to solve the problem of untouchability. The change of physical and material condition of untouchables is not enough.

References

G. Shah, H. Mander, S. Thorat, S. Deshpande, A. Baviskar. (2006). *Untouchability in Rural India*, New Delhi: Sage Publications.

Pitrim Sorokin.(1927). *Social Mobility*. New York: Harper and Brothers.

S. M. Michael. (1999). *Untouchable, Dalits in Modern India*, New Delhi: Sage Publications .

Sanjay Kumar, Anthony Heath, Oliver Heath, "Determinants of Social Mobility in India", *Economic and Political Weekly*, vol. 37, no. 29, 2002.

Smita Narula. "Equal by Law, Unequal by Caste: The "Untouchable" Condition in Critical Race Perspective" *Wisconsin International Law Journal*, vol. 26, 2007.

THEORETICAL FRAMEWORK TO ASSESS THE IMPACT OF ECONOMIC REFORMS ON SCHEDULE CASTE IN GUJARAT

Dr. Naresh M Chauhan

Project Director-ICSSR sponsored Research Project, SC Study, Gujarat and Assistant Professor, Department of Rural Economics, Gujarat Vidyapith, Ahmedabad

Abstract

In India Schedule caste is defined as one of the most marginalized groups which required special attention from the State and society. The schedule castes face multiple exclusions in Indian society, so that the impact of various state policies would probably vary for these castes groups than the remaining groups of the society in India. This research paper deals with to develop the theoretical framework to assess the impact of economic reforms in Gujarat for these schedule castes group. In this paper first of all, I described the multiple exclusion which schedule castes faces in Indian society, with the help of some previous studies. In second phase the economic reforms and their impact in general is mentioned. After define economic reforms affected areas (in multidimensional) in third phase, in fourth phase I derived the multidimensional theoretical frame for schedule castes groups, which can assess the impact of economic reforms in Gujarat. In Indian society the schedule castes are not in a homogeneous characteristics, the special characteristics of schedule castes in Gujarat is also identified in this segment and how the derived theoretical framework has taken in to account these characters is also discussed. This derived theoretical framework addressed all the segment of human life with special requirement of schedule castes in Gujarat. It consist the impact of economic reforms on livelihood, health, education, consumption patterns etc. the derived framework is a Wholistic view, it can assess the impact of economic reforms in general as a sum of various segmented impacts in multiple dimensions. Finally the article also identified some measurable indicators from these probable affected areas, which would be make possible quantifiable assessment of economic reforms' impact on schedule cases in Gujarat.

Introduction

The Indian society contains the different socio-economic classes with inherited castes and communities. The process of socio-economic transformation of society (Especially after the economic reforms in India) is not neutral for all class and castes. Hence the deep concern arises regarding 'Inclusive growth' (social/economic/socio-economic exclusion) for particular caste and classes of the society (within the Gujarat state). This article is about to identify the major areas of concern among the different groups of the society. The proposed framework is about to drafting the major areas and highlighting the major concerns regarding effect made by economic reforms. This framework is just primary attempt and one should mind that there are tremendous scope for omission and additions in this framework.

Economic Reforms in India in brief

As we know that India adopt the liberal economic policy in 1991, which is generally known as LPG that is about 'L' stand for liberalization, 'P' stand for privatization and 'G' stand for globalization. These new economic policies contain 'market friendly' steeps. This policy is also known as "U-turn" policy. The entirely this policies mix carried out by economic reforms.

Schedule caste in Brief

Schedule castes contain those castes which are considered as 'Untouchable" in Indian caste system. These castes are considered as Schedule caste in constitution of India to provide them special treatment.

Why need of separate theoretical framework for Schedule Caste to assess the Impact of Economic Reforms

Economic reforms of 1991 in India is about the shrink the government role in the economy and providing more space to market, hence the role of care taker of economically weaker section by the State is also shrink. The schedule castes are mostly economical weaker sections but they are required some special treatment through the Government sectors as they are consider 'Untouchables' or 'Non preferable'. So that they will suffer worse, in case of role of state shrink. Liberal market functions with the situation of caste system prevailing in society required special consideration of those Schedule castes with special frame work in this regard.

Why Gujarat required separate theoretical framework?

Gujarat has leading industrial society but the same time it is also proved a society with leading caste conservative society. As the Gujarat is highly industrialized state, it is affected highly with economic reforms and it is considered as a faster developing state in compare of other states of India. Gujarat is also consider as a poor health, education and livelihood providing to its' weaker section in India. To examine the current situation this paper deals only with Gujarat with take in to consideration its special requirement with focus of health, education and livelihood areas.

Uses of proposed theoretical framework

i. To determine/to identify the Whollistic standard of living of SCs' as well as Non SCs'.

ii. To measure general standard of living (as an aggregate standard of living for entire state)

iii. To compare the standard of living of particular sub caste's within the SCs.

iv. To find out the variation of standard of living among the various groups of SCs.

v. Helpful to find out relation within the particular class (or sub caste) for their progressive or poor performance.

vi. Helpful to investigate the role of government in case of each class for their progressive or poor performance.

vii. Helpful to investigate the role of government (various promotional programs) to improve the standard of living among the various groups of the SCs.

viii. To dissections the various factors which determine the standard of life and to find out the strength and weakness factors for each groups of the society.

Broad areas which affected directly through economic reforms in Gujarat

The policy of economic reforms applied in India is affected broadly in entire society, but one of the major outcome of this economic policy is about shrink of government that affect some of the weaker section more than the other specially the weaker groups of schedule castes are affected much more than the other but that hypothesis is also prevailing similar for other weaker section in the country. Now as we all know that Gujarat is one of the higher caste discrimination prone state, here the entire situation would be worsen, on the one hand the state's role of care taker shrink (that makes weaker worse off) and the other hand the expanding market would not providing equal opportunities to those of scheduled castes. The following figure illustrated the hypothesis of how caste system and shrinking state role affect the schedule caste worse. The funnel represents the shrinking state's role within the caste system which shrinks the opportunities of schedule caste. As far as this frame work consider the Whollistic approach, we consider them as area of Education, health, livelihood and special treatment for vulnerable section providing by government.

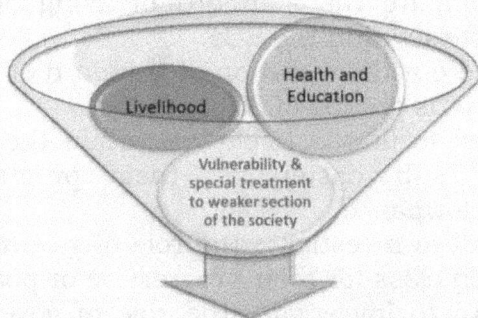

Caste system and shrinking state's role resulting shrinking SCs opportunities

Figure 1 Caste system and shrinking government's role shrinking SCs' opportunities

32

Broad Areas Covered Under the Health Sector

The discourse regarding poor health performance of Gujarat is going on in various researches reports and Medias as far as this theoretical framework concern this is an attempt to investigation the realities with reference of schedule castes in Gujarat after the policy of economic reforms.

The following figure-2 is about the broad areas covered under the health sector, which include the factors depicting in the figure-2. To assess the effect of economic reforms on schedule castes the theoretical framework illustrated in figure-2 helps to investigate in all various direction which would be give us multidimensional picture of the health sectors.

The framework for health status contain total five major dimensions are as following:

(A) Health expenditures in various health inputs
(B) Health Infrastructure
(C) Morbidity indicators
(D) Mortalities rates
(E) Reproductive Health Status

The areas and indictors for each dimension are described briefly following the figure-2.

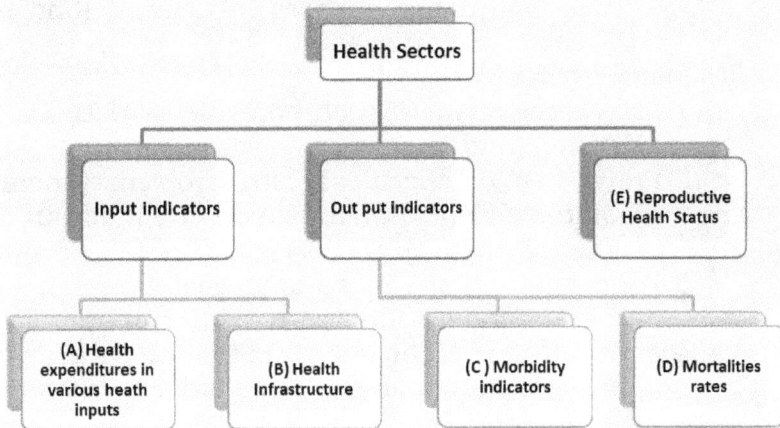

Figure 2 Framework for Wholistic health status assessment

33

(A) Health expenditures in various health inputs
1. Health expenditure as a percentage of total revenue expenditure (find out the caste wise utilization)
2. Per capita government health expenditure (find out the caste wise utilization)
3. Health expenditure on area specific requirements (leptospyrosis, sycalcell, phileria etc for south Gujarat region) (find out the caste wise utilization)
4. Health expenditure in absolute terms (revenue as well as health capital expenditure)   etc. (find out the caste wise)

(B) Health Infrastructure
1. 1.   Numbers of Hospitals/Dispensaries /PHC/CHC per lacks of population etc. (find out the caste wise utilization)
2. Numbers of beds per lacks of population etc. (find out the caste wise utilization)
3. Availability of Medical and paramedical staff/ lacks of population (Allopathic/ Aayurvedic/ Homeopathy etc) (find out the caste wise utilization)
4. Utilization of medical emergencies services (108- ambulance services in district) (find out the caste wise utilization)

(C) Morbidity indicators
1. Prevalence of specific (chronic) dieses (T.B, AIDS/ HIV etc) (find out the caste wise figure)
2. Prevalence of specific health problem (Anemia, Iodine deficiency, Malnutrition etc) (find out the caste wise figure)
3. Performance data of various goal based health program(find out the caste wise figure)
4. Acute health problems (Numbers of patients for different acute dieses. Etc (find out the caste wise figure)

(D) Mortalities rates (find out the caste wise figure)
IMR/ CDR/ ASMR/ PNMR/NMR/ SBR etc(find out the caste wise figure)

1.   Prevalence of dieses specific deaths. Etc(find out the caste wise figure)

(E) Reproductive Health Status (find out the caste wise figure)
　　　　1.CBR/ ASFR/ GFR etc
　　　　2.Institutional delivery
　　　　3.Nutritional indicators for pregnant and lactating women etc.
　　　　4.*"Angan-wadi"* and child nutritional programs
　　　　5.Various immunization programs for children's/ vaccination programs
　　　　6.Overall Mother-Infant health measures. Etc
The frame work provide that these are the areas where the differentiations would be occurring between the Schedule castes and Non Schedule caste, likewise the board areas regarding livelihood is mention in figure-3 as following.

Broad Areas Covered Under the livelihood/ Employment opportunities

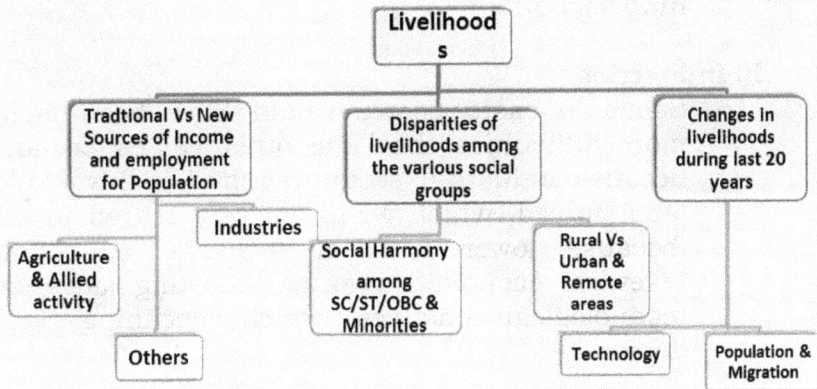

Figure 3 Broad Areas Covered Under the livelihood

Schedule castes are fundamentally economic backward class moreover they provided lower social status so that they are basically excluded from the main stream economic activities in previous centuries. In lack of higher productive economic activity they are living in poor conditions. The figure-3 provide the frame to assess the impact of economic reforms by classify the areas where SCs are suppose to affect differ than the others.

A. Traditional Vs New Sources of Income and employment for Population

i. **Agriculture & Allied activity:** Economic reforms have been changed entire scenario of economic activities. Schedule castes people are performed as laborer from the beginning because Indian caste system did not allowed them to perform as the sources of other than labor. Economic reforms has changed role of labor, moreover reforms content labor law reforms also. Labor reforms contain lower job security with higher efficiencies/ responsibilities. Such working environment most probably make Schedule caste people excluded from the better job opportunities which is determine by prejudiced elements within the market forces. Such factors also should be taken in to account.

ii. Industries

Schedule caste people would have been facing more difficulties than the other castes because, because industrial sector required highly skilled labor forced, which would be very scared in SCs (because lower level of technical education). Likewise economic reforms boosting advanced technological changes which declining labor demand.

iii. Others

Some other issue regarding livelihood like hazardous working environment, traditional and small scale industries shrinking etc should also consider in this section, in which SCs' of Gujarat might have face much more difficulties than the others.

36

B. Disparities of livelihoods among the various social groups

i. **Social Harmony among SC/ST/OBC & Minorities**

Throat cutting competition in professional life under the influence of economic reforms would make man much more prejudice than ever before. How the SCs would have been performing in non harmonious environment should address in this section.

ii. **Rural Vs Urban & Remote areas**

Schedule caste people who living in urban locality are facing lower huddles even post economic era but large portion of SCs are living in urban and remote areas what are the changes they face should also consider in this segment.

C. Changes in livelihoods during last 20 years

i. **Technology:**

What are the changes made by economic reforms and whether these changes are caste free or not in Gujarat? This question would be investigating separately.

ii. **Population & Migration:**

Livelihood status also determine by level of population and migration of population so that what happen in this regards in Gujarat since last 20 years should be taken in to account.

Areas of Education and SCs in Gujarat after Economic reforms

Human development determine by level of education, which is mostly affected under the economic reforms. In this new educational environment how Schedule caste people affected can be assess with the following frame work in which broad Areas Covered, hence there would be some specific issues that might be address independently.

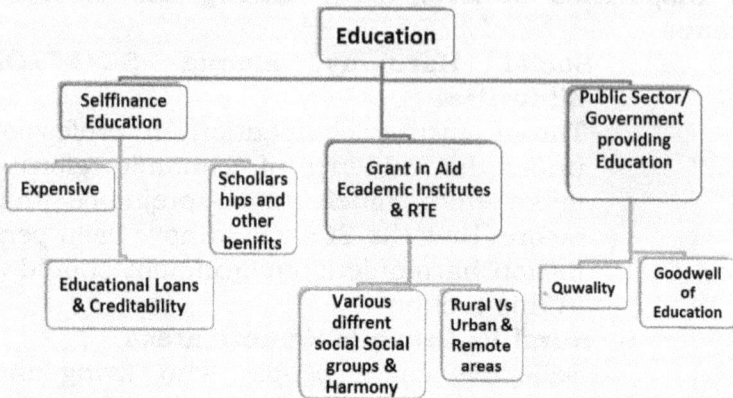

Figure 4 Broad Areas covered Under the Education to assese the effect of economic reforms on SCs

Under educational area there should be considered following questions:

  a) Self-finance Education which is promoted and boosting by economic reforms

      1) Expensive education and difficulties facing by economic weaker and how the difficulties facing by SCs?

      2) Educational Loans & Creditability: whether creditability to access the educational loan is identical for SCs and Non SCs' are equal or not? Should be investigating.

      3) Scholarships and other benefits. Whether scholarship and other benefits are increasing as per requirement of newer scenario for SCs should also consider.

  b) Grant in Aid Academic Institutes & Right to Education (RTE)

      1) Various different social groups & Harmony: grant in aid educational institutes are providing somewhat quality education but how much portion of SCs can access those facility and whether those are in lower percentage than the Non SCs or Not? Weather the implementation RTE provides the equal scope for SCs or Not?

and how economic reforms affected the situation in Gujarat? Such questions can discuss in this section.

2) Rural Vs Urban & Remote areas: Our general observation shows that rural areas have higher caste discrimination than the urban in general, so that what is the scenario in rural urban educational institute and whether there are discrimination prevails and how economic reforms effect the situation that also should be consider

c) Public Sector/ Government providing Education

1) Quality of public education in post economic reforms in Gujarat and

2) Goodwill of public education in post economic reforms in Gujarat

Such area should also be focused so that we can discuss how a large portion of economic weaker class (contained large number of SCs) which is dependent of public sector's education system affects by economic reforms.

Other Areas of concern: according to this theoretical framework there would be some other areas as following which also require special attention.

1. Rural Urban disparities and worsen the SCs' situation in post economic reforms
2. Disparities among the different sub caste within the SCs'
3. Issues of Exclusion/Inclusion in general sense.

Help to assessment of affect of economic reforms on Schedule caste

There is a large spread spectrum of standard of living prevails within the different groups of the society, broadly it is classified as (i) Inter variation: Between SC and Non SC groups of the society and (ii) Intra variation: difference between the different section of the same group also prevails in this regards as they are not homogeneous groups. In such reality there are basic questions in this regards are as:

I. **How to measure these differences of Whollistic standard of living accurately?**

To measure these differences; the multidimensional approach (Whollistic standard of living) is required. This proposed theoretical framework helps to measure the Whollistic standard of living with the help of operation definition of standard of living.

II. **How to define multidimensional/ Whollistic standard of living, which can focus on the differences prevails between various groups of the society?**

Various government finance (whether these are in forms of subsidies/ affirmative programs) influence differently to the different groups of the society. The proposed theoretical framework helps to measurement/ assesses these differences. This proposed framework also suggests analyzing what are the government's financial supports and their output (weather these are in forms of subsidies/ affirmative programs) to each group of the society? Is there any difference among the various groups of the society in the regards of cost benefit analysis of government financial supports? If 'yes' than why?

Proposed Research Method of Index building:
Such study would be on the basis of various combination of primary and secondary data base. Primary data will be depending on the sample survey which would be collected in case of lack of required data.
The entire research methods are divided in following steps.

i. Measurement of 'Whollistic standard of living': To determine/to identify the Whollistic standard of living: As we know the phenomena of Whollistic standard of living is a multidimensional, this theoretical framework helps us to identification of appropriate/suitable dimensions in second phase we can design set of the appropriate indicators to measure all the directions which influence Whollistic standard of living. Set of indictors for various dimensions like health, education, livelihood etc.

ii. Aggregated 'Whollistic standard of living' for particular group of the society: with the help of concern literature and our proposed theoretical framework we can design 'composite index' for each groups like SCs and Non SCs, in same way we can also prepare it for base time period (T0) as well as comparable time(T1). To find out the average (weight will be provided to each indices indicator as per there importance) of indices of indexes we can get the composite index for each groups of the society, which will gave us the situation of different social groups for that particular point of time. With the help of this dimensional composite indexes we will be calculate the Whollistic standard of living that would be the compilation of all dimensional composite indexes.

iii. Measurement of composite index in post economic reforms and pre economic reforms for each group of the society we can compare both the situation and can assess the impact of globalization on the particular groups of SCs.

Possibilities of study to measure the impact on SCs

1. Static analysis (Post reforms impact measurement)
Static analysis is about to measure the differences between the two groups of SCs' Vs Non SCs' that can provide us the picture regarding what is the differences prevails between these two groups (at a particular point of time). The static analysis is Ex-post analysis by nature. There would be a no difference between these two groups as well as there would be a minor disparities as well as major disparities between these two groups. The following two figures show these two situations in example (potential). The minor and major differences are subject to definition of researcher. The indicators are converted in a index forms and figures are illustrate those index values.

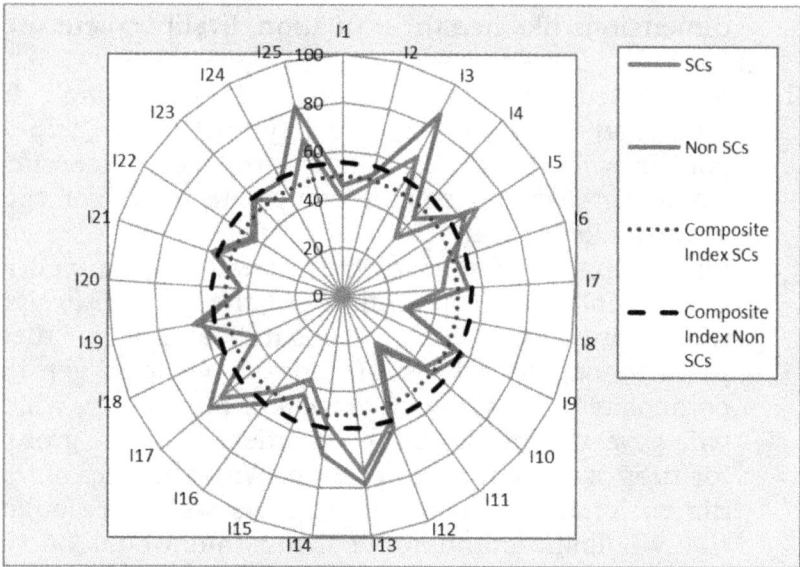

Figure 5 Possibilities of Minor differences between SCs' and Non SCs' in static analysis

Figure-5 depicted the possibility of minor differences between the SCs' and Non SCs' groups the two dashed lines (which shows Whollistic performance or aggregated performance of the group) closer to each other that indicate comparatively lower differences between these two groups. However the differences are subjective, to define higher or lower is contextual matter. In this example we if we assume or define figure-5 as a minor/lower differences so that in compare of figure-6 we can say that would be higher or major/higher differences.

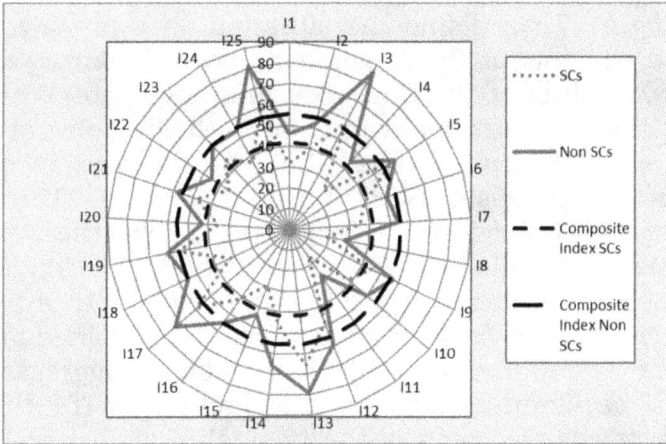

Figure 6 Possibilities of major differences between SCs' and Non SCs'

1. Dynamic Analysis:

Static analysis is not providing the entire picture of changing society. To measure the changing scenario we should have a dynamic analysis. Simply we can say dynamic analysis is about to illustrate two different results of static analysis of same groups in a single platform. Which is depicted in figure-7 and 8 as below?

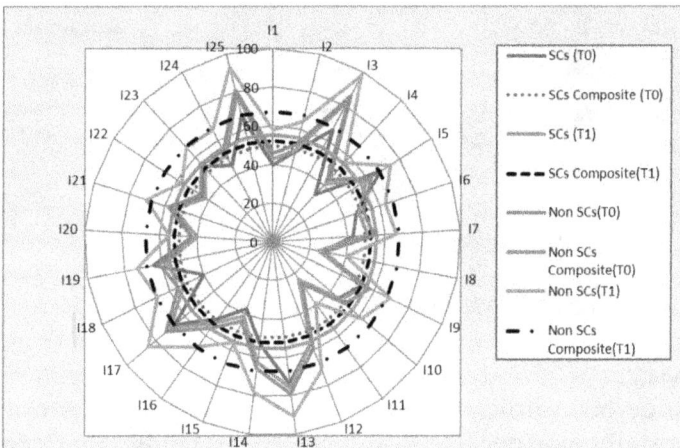

Figure 7 Possibility of pro inequality growth

In figure-7 we define the situation as a pro inequality because the inequality is going to be a widening during these two points of the time (See the aggregate/Whollistic dashed line for both the groups for both the point of time). in figure-7 we can see that the situation of inequality between two groups of SCs' Vs Non SCs' at T0 (T0 time is consider as a pre reform period) is lower than the situation of inequality prevails at the T1 time period. (T1 time is post reform). In same order figure-8 is consider as a pro equity growth because in figure-8 we can see that the inequality at T0 time is reduced and the Whollistic or aggregate line seem to be identical for both the groups for T1 time, in another words we can say the inequality abolished by the growth process so such growth process would be consider as a pro equity growth.

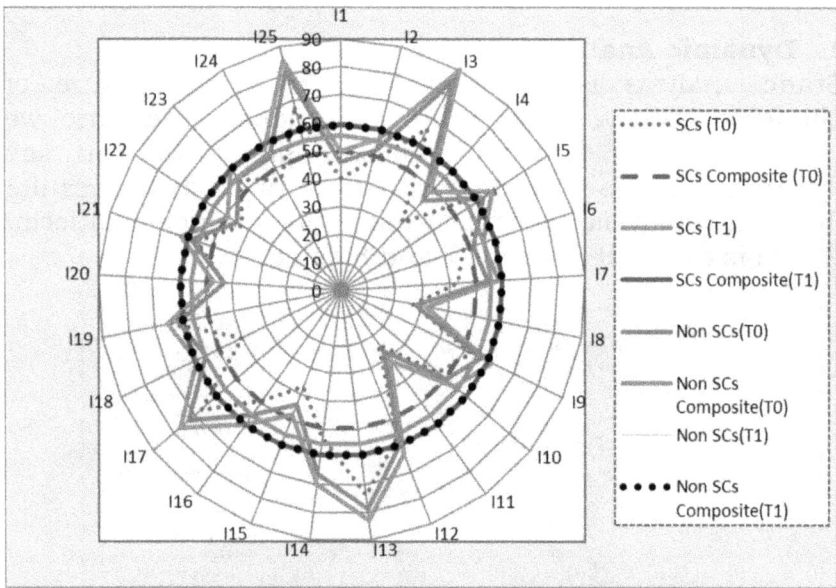

Figure 8 Possibility of pro equality growth

Summary

Hence economic reforms are not affecting SCs and Non SCs' equally is the fundamental hypothesis, how can we measure the impact on SCs and Non SCs'? This question is solved through measurement of Whollistic standard of living in this proposed theoretical framework. The major question would be arise why Gujarat should have a different theoretical frame work in this regards the simple answer is ; every place and each time should have different theoretical frame work to capture the specific issues at specific time. In this frame work we have selected the areas or dimensions which Gujarat required to measure the most.

INFLUENCE OF RELIGION AND SOCIAL STIGMA ININDIAN POLITICS

Dr. Dinesh S. Parmar
Head
Department of Political Science
Shree N.M.Shah Arts and Comm. College
Shankheshwar, Dist: Patan. (N.G.)

Abstract

India is a democratic republic and also a home of innumerable caste, class, religion and creed. **Vasudhaiv Kutumbakam** *is India's vibrancy. But today, religion has now become a debatable issue. Politics of any nation depends on its social background. Generally, language, caste, religion, class and creed etc. are the social elements, which can be called the formative influences in the formation of politics of a nation. India is a home of many religions like Hindu, Muslim, Christian, Sikh, Parsi, Buddhist, etc. Since time immemorial, India had been remained a host and home of the religions of the world. All these religions immensely contributed in the Indian society. Their influence cannot be ignored. The history of India is replete with the occurrences and incidents of communal violence between Hindu and Muslim etc. In short, communalism is a contemporary anarchist philosophy based on the religious orthodoxy. The small minority communities must cultivate compassion, faith and trust to the majority community. We all should try to solve the problem through the social engineering and also with the help of religion which does not divide but which joins the people.*

Keywords: Religion, Social stigma, politics, communalism, race, creed, India and Pakistan, tolerance

Introduction

Politics of any nation depends on its social background. Generally, language, caste, religion, class and creed etc. are the social elements, which can be called the formative influences in the formation of politics of a nation. India is a home of many religions like Hindu, Muslim, Christian, Sikh, Parsi, Buddhist, etc. since time immemorial, India had been remained a host and home of the religions of the world. All these religions immensely contributed in the Indian society. Their influence cannot be ignored. We all know that social life flourished from the feeling of co-existence of people of various class and creed. India is a democratic nation so we have accepted the principal of equality. Religion or *Dharma* is a matter of man's innate belief and faith. But at the same time, religion plays a key role in nation's politics and social life. Sometimes, it becomes an indispensible and deciding factor, or a cause of the social stigma. Society is a web of social relations.[1] According to Collins Dictionary; Stigma is a distinguishing mark of social disgrace.[2] According to Wikipedia;

Social stigma is the extreme disapproval of (or discontent with) a person or group on socially characteristic grounds that are perceived, and serve to distinguish them, from other members of a society. Stigma may then be affixed to such a person, by the greater society, who differs from their cultural norms.[3]

In a religious state, religion is a part of our social life, but even in secular state, religion plays a major role in the currents of politics. According to Kingsley Devis; "Religion is so universal, stable and solid that we cannot understand human society without the clear understanding of religion." The history of India is replete with the occurrences and incidents of communal violence between Hindu and Muslim etc. according to the Encyclopedia of Political Science:

In Indian politics, some people's selfish tendency to give importance, benefits to their own caste, race and religion, to keep good relations only with them, this kind of tendency creates agitation and feeling of hatred in other religions. This kind of opposition sometime converts into communalism and communal riots.[4]

In short, communalism is a contemporary anarchist philosophy based on the religious orthodoxy. Communalism believes in the philosophy that the people who follow one religion, their interest should be equal and collective. In India, before 15th century to 10th century, it was the period of Hindu dominance, after 10th century, the Muslim period started and till 1857 the Mogul rule continued without any pause. During this period, the Muslim rule accelerated the religious conversion process. This further widened the gap between two religions and the feeling of social stigma increased between them. Thus, the feeling that the traditions and rituals of both the religions are different and they are against each other. Mohammed Iqubal and Mohd. Ali Jinnah advocated two nation theory on the basis of religion. Thus, Hindustan got divided into two different states; India and Pakistan. In 1906, Jinnah advocated separate voting right for the Muslims, formation of Muslim League etc. These incidents are the outcome of the social stigma between these two religions. In the Muslim League meeting in 1940, Jinnah said that;

Hindus and the Muslims are different races, their traditions, rituals, customs and social systems are different. So, both are separate people. That is why they should live in separate nations.[5]

In India, Hindu nationalism versus Muslim separatism was the cause of social stigma between these two religions. This poisonous influence increased in India even though Gandhiji's epic struggle against communalism and casteism, during and after independence. Incidents of communal violence were continued in India. All the major studies regarding political and social sciences underestimated or not studied carefully the impact of religion in the major incidents like Indo-Pak war of 1965, 1971, and Kargil war, the Pakistan supported cross border terrorism and subsequent violent events of Ayodhya, Akshardham, Godhara, and Anti-Sikh riots of 1984. These major and minor incidents of communal violence have raised many questions against the secular state of India.

48

Prof. Rajani Kothari vehemently says;

With the incident of 06th December, 1992, our hope for the secular state based on the Hindu, Muslim, Sikh, Christian brotherhood was broken.[6]

Today, India is divided in many communal and religious groups which helps or motivates communal politics. The recent incidents of religious conversion, the religious polarization promoted by political parties, poor economical condition, communal havoc instigated by religious priests are the main factors responsible for the social sigma in Indian politics. The political parties motivated the communalism between these religions and thus the feeling of social stigma aroused. The voting system, choice of electoral candidates and ministers was depended on the caste and religion. Sometimes governmental machinery and policies are becomes the root of social-religious stigma.

The conflict arises between the Hindus and Christians because of the foreign funding to the Christian missionaries and their unlawful conversion. The Christian missionaries converted the Hindu minorities like Schedule Caste and Schedule Tribes, this further increased in the conflict between the Hindus and the Christians. The demand of separate Khalistan and later killings of the Sikhs was the result of the social stigma created and encouraged by the religious elements. The recent conversion of the Muslims *'Ghar Vapsi'* is also an event of the same chain. This Muslim conversion should not be our revenge for the age-old historical Hindu conversion.

To conclude, we can say that we have to create consciousness against communal elements that creates social stigma and thus pollutes political system. We should bring the change in the approach and mentality of the political parties. Our political parties should rule the country without any communal approach or interests.

After Independence, in the Hindus and the Muslims, there lies in depth social relations between them and these relations are still existed.[7]

Thus, the small minority communities must cultivate compassion, faith and trust to the majority community. We all should try to solve the problem through the social engineering and also with the help of religion which does not divide but which joins the people. The true sense of religion is in tolerance and not in division. The vision of a state should be in the sense of *Rajdharma*. 'TIT FOT TAT' is not the final solution for any healthy political system. This is the need of the time that we should cultivate all inclusive and positive approach in education, media and governance.

References

1. McIver. R.M. And Page C.H. : Society (1953) p.g.01
2. http://www.collinsdictionary.com/dictionary/english/stigma
3. http://en.wikipedia.org/wiki/Social_stigma
4. Shukla Gajendra. Bhartiya Rajakaran. Popular Prakashan, 2010-11, p.g.222
5. Shukla Dinesh And Amin Hasmukh. Bharatiya Rajakaran Ni Ruprekha. Gujarat University Granth Nirman Board, 1972, p.g.37.
6. Kothari Rajani. Bharatiya Rajakaran ma Komvad. Rainbow Publishers, New Delhi, 2002. p.g.87.
7. Sheth Pravin And Shukla Dinesh. Bharat Nu Rajakaran. Gujarat University Granth Nirman Board, 1972, p.g.76.

TRIBAL DEVELOPMENT ISSUES IN INDIA : SOME OBSERVATION

Kamlesh P. Dabhi

Associate Professor, L.D. Arts College, Ahmedabad

Introduction

The largest concentration of tribal communities in the world, next to Africa is in India. The tribal are the weakest of the weaker section in India. It was only after the country became independence that a clear policy in regard to tribal welfare and development emerged. While the integration of the tribals with rest of the society in India was considered in imperative of nation building in extending to them the benefits of development every efforts was to be, made to preserve their distinctive life styles. The commitment to bribal welfare is built into the constitution of India itself which provides for an elaborate framework for socio-economic development of scheduled tribes and for preventing their exploitation by other groups of society. Scheduled V and VI of the constitution provide the basic contours of the constitutional scheme for the protection of schedules tribes and the administration of scheduled areas. Beside, the constitution has also spelt out a number of review monitoring and watch-dog mechanisms. The constitution also reserve a number of seats for scheduled tribes in the service and posts of union and state government.

The Scheduled Tribe

A multiplicity of names is used in various countries to identify such group of people. For example "Native Americans' and "Pacific Islander" in the Unites States, 'Inuit', Metis and 'First Nations', in Canada; 'Aborigines in Australia, "Hill Tribes" in South East Asia; indigenous ethnic minorities, "Schedules Tribes; or Adivasi in India etc.

The English term "Tribe is derived from the Latin word 'tribus' to mean "A group of persons forming a community and claiming descent from a common anscestor (Fried, 1975). According to Prof. Majumdar "A tribe is a social group with territorial affiliation, endogamous with no specialization of functions, rules by tribal officers, hereditary or otherwise, united in language or dialect, recognizing social distance from tribes or castes, but without any stigma attached in the case of caste structure, following tribal traditions, beliefs and customs, illiberal of naturalization of ideas from alien sources, above all conscious of a homogeneity of ethnic and territorial integration".

Tribal communities of India are commonly referred to as tribal or 'adivasi' and are recognized as 'scheduled tribes' under the constittuion of India. Although the word 'Tribe' or 'Tribal' is not defined anywhere in the constitution of India but Article 366 (25) refers to scheduled tribes as those communities who are scheduled in accordance with Article 342 of the constitution of India. Article 342 of the constitution states that the 'scheduled tribes' are the tribes or tribal communities or part of or groups within these tribes, which have been declared as such by the president through a public notification.

Objectives
The main objectives of this paper are :
1. To understand tribal community and regional distribution.
2. To highlight various demographic profile of tribes.
3. Constitutional provision for tribes in India.
4. Tribal development status and issues in India.

Tribal Community of India and its Regional Distribution
These tribals are not homogenous groups and live in varied ecological and climatic conditions ranging from plains and forest hills to inaccessible areas. The tribals constitute the second largest social group of India and accounts for about 9% of the total population of India. Their

population has grown at the growth rate of 24.45% during the last one-decade census.

The tribal population live in about 15% of the India's area. Largely unaffected by modern world, they are very simple and often curious people who have retained their rituals and customs. Among them about 80 per cent live in the central belt, extending from Gujarat (8.87%) and Rajasthan in west, and across the State of Maharashtra, Madhya Pradesh, Chattisgarh, Bihar, Jharkhand and Orissa to West Bengal and Tripura in the East. Most of the remaining 20 per cent live in the Northeastern states of Meghalaya, Mizoram, Nagaland, Arunachal Pradesh and Sikkim and in the union territories of Dadara and Nagar Haveli Andaman and Nicobar and Lakshsdweep. A few of them live in Southern States of Kerala, Tamil Nadu and Karnataka, Andhra Pradesh has the largest tribal population among the southern states of India. Thus The tribal population is scattered in all states and union territories in India except for the state of Haryana, Punjab, Delhi and Chandigarh.

More than 700 scheduled tribes are notified under article 342 of the constitutional India, each with distinct cultures, social practices, religions dialects and occupations (Ministry of Tribal Affairs, 2009).

The characteristics of traditional tribal communities are as follows:
  ➢ All the tribal people have a very close attachment to the territory that they have been living in. These territories are in relative geographical isolation. This locational isolation is also cause of the discrimination largely carried out by the main stream population (D'souza 2003)
  ➢ Most of the tribal population in the forest of India live in areas that are rich in natural resources. They are largely dependent on natural resources for their survival.

> The tribals represent distinct culture group. The tribals have their own language and they have their own culture that is very different and unique from that of the other groups of the population.

> In spite of the various problems, they do have their own social and political institutions and live a life that is full of rituals and other tradition. They are more community oriented.

> Land and other natural resources are considered non exploitative and are respected.

♦ **To highlight various demographic profile of tribes.**

(a) Trends of Tribal Population

Table-1 Trend in General and ST population 1951-2001 in Millions.

Census year	Total Pop	ST Pop	Prop of ST Pop (%)	Decadal Growth rate ST	Decadal Gr. of on SC/St pop.
1951	356.8	19.1	5.4		
1961	439.2	30.1	6.9	57.6	20.4
1971	547.9	38.0	6.9	26.2	24.7
1981	665.3	51.6	7.8	35.8	18.4
1991	838.6	67.8	8.1	31.2	24.3
2001	1028.6	84.3	8.2	24.5	22.9

Source : Census of India : 1951, 1961, 1971, 1981, 2001.

Overall increasing trend is observed for both general population and scheduled tribe. Percentage of scheduled tribe population to the total population has increased from 5.4% in 1951 to 8.2 in 2001. Decadal growth rate of scheduled tribe population is higher compared to growth rate of general population (B Sureshlal-2014)

(b) Sex Ratios (Sex Composition)

Table-2 Sex ratio of general population and scheduled tribe : 1961 – 2001 (Sex Ratio : No. of female per 1000 males)

Census Year	Total Population	Scheduled Tribe
1961	941	987
1971	930	982
1981	934	984
1991	927	972
2001	933	978

Source : Census of India 1961, 1971, 1981, 2001 series-I India, part + 2B primary census abstract (ST).

As compared to general population, there appears to be more even distribution of male and females among the scheduled Tribes, Sex Ratio of scheduled tribes are relatively higher than that of general population. This suggests that females in the tribal society are not neglected. The social and cultural values protected their interest. But is stated to show declining trend from 982 in 1971 to 972 in 1991 again it has increased slightly to 978 in 2001, this decline could be attributed to higher morality amongst females of scheduled tribe community due to their nutritional deficiency and limited access to health service. Slight increase in 2001 may be the positive impact of special health and family welfare drive for them (Table-2).

(c) Rate of Literary

Table-3 Literary Rate among General and Scheduled Tribe Population:

Particular	General Population			Scheduled Population		
	1981	1991	2001	1981	1991	2001
Total	36.23	52.21	65.38	16.35	26.23	47.10
Male	46.80	64.13	75.3	24.52	32.50	59.17
Female	24.82	39.28	54.16	8.04	14.50	34.76

The level of literary is the one of the most important indicators of social, culture and health improvement among

Tribal communities (Madan 1951) By and large their response to programmes of literary and of formal education varied significantly between tribes and regions. Female literary is a powerful instrument for social change female literary among tribals is low compared to general population (Chauhan, 1990) literary rate for ST male and female register increasing trend during 1981 to 2001, but there is a wide gap between general population and scheduled tribe population with respect to literary rate females literary for scheduled tribe is still very low (Table-3)

(d) Distribution of Age

Table-4 Age distribution and dependency ratio of scheduled tribe and non-scheduled tribe population : 2001

Particular	Scheduled Tribe	Non-Scheduled Tribe
Age distribution		
0-14	39.52	35.08
15-59	54.38	57.33
60+	6.10	7.59
Total	100	100
Dependency Ratio	83.89	74.43
Aging Index : Total	15.43	21.64
Male	14.28	20.49
Female	16.62	22.90

Source : Census of India 2001, social and cultural table.

Age distribution provide population characteristics of any region of sub-population it can indicate whether population structure is young or old. See the (table-4) it can be presumed that tribal population is relatively younger than non-tribal population in the age group 0-14 (younger population) is about 40% whereas for non scheduled tribe population it is 35% as per 2001 census. Aging Index is lower for scheduled tribe 15%. Compared to non scheduled tribe 22% proportion economically active population (15-59 age group) is lower compared to non-tribe population.

Dependency ratio is much higher for scheduled tribe 84% whereas for non-tribe it is 74%.

(e) Educational Status

Table-5 Cross enrolment Ratio of scheduled Tribes and total population (1990-91 to 1999-2000)

Particular		1990-1991		1999-2000	
Year classes		I to V	I to VIII	I to V	I to VIII
Total Population	Total	100.1	62.1	94.9	58.8
	Boys	114.0	76.6	104.1	67.2
	Girls	85.5	47.8	85.2	49.7
Scheduled Tribes	Total	103.4	39.7	97.7	58.0
	Boys	126.8	51.3	112.7	70.8
	Girls	78.6	27.5	82.7	44.8
Gap	Total	(+)3.3	(-) 22.4	(+) 2.8	(-) 0.8
	Boys	(+) 12.8	(-) 25.3	(+) 8.6	(+) 3.6
	Girls	(-) 6.9	(-) 20.3	(-) 2.5	(-) 4.9

Source : Annual Report of Respective Years. Department of Education, Ministry of Human Resource Development GOI, New Delhi.

Efforts of universalizing primary education continued through the programme of Sarva Shiksha Abhiyan. The national programme of Nutritional support to primary education or the Midday Meal act as a support service to increase retention rate. The pace of progress of enrolment of both scheduled tribe boys and girls at the middle level has been quite impressive. As compared to that of total population scheduled tribe girls maintained a good pace, especially at the middle level. However enrolment ratio for scheduled tribe girls both at primary and middle levels was lower that the total population in both years.

(f) Table-6 Drop Out Rate amongst Scheduled Tribes and Total Population (1990-91 to 1992-2000)

Category	Class-V		Classes-I-VIII		Classes (I to X)	
	1990-91	1998-99	1990-91	1998-99	1990-91	1998-99
Total	42.60	39.74	60.90	56.82	71.34	67.44
STs	62.52	57.36	78.57	72.80	85.01	82.96
Gap	19.92	17.62	17.67	15.98	13.67	15.52

Source : Education profile of states, Department of Education, Ministry of Human Resource Development GOI, New Delhi.

The problem of drop out happens to be a common features for both general and scheduled trend student. While both the categories have been showing a decreasing trend during 1990-91 to 1998-99, the problem still appear to be the worst with regard to schedule tribe as they classes 1 to 8 and 82.96 in classes 1 to 10 during 1998-99. Also the gap between the general population and scheduled tribe was found to be widening from 13.67 in 1990-91 to 15.52 in 1998-99 at the secondary level which is a cause for much concern.

♦ **Constitutional Status of tribes in India**
The constitution of India provides for a comprehensive framework for the socio-economic development of scheduled tribes and for preventing them for exploitation and injustice. It provides necessary safeguard for the right of tribal people under various Articles and Laws. Let us see it

- Article 46 of the "directive principles of the state policy" which are fundamental in the governance of country" states:

There shall promote with special care the educational and economic interest of the weaker sections of the people, and in particular of the scheduled castes and the scheduled tribes and shall protect them from social injustice and all from of exploitation.

- Article 342 empower the president to specify "the tribes or tribal communities, or parts of or groups within tribes or the "tribal communities" to be notified as scheduled tribes within a state or a union territory.
- As for tribal habitats, areas having substantial tribal population have been notified as Tribal Areas in the north eastern states under the sixth scheduled and as a scheduled area in the rest of the country under the Fifth schedule as provided under Article 244.
- Article 275 (1) takes care of the financial requirement of tribal development. All schemes made to raise the level of administration and approved by the Government of India, Secure automatic sanctions being a change on the consolidation fund of India. However unfortunately in actual practice, the financial arrangement contemplated under this article, remained inoperative till very recently.
- Articles 330 and 322 provide for reservation of seats for scheduled castes and scheduled tribes in the parliament and state legislative assembly.
- Article 335 stipulates reservation in service.
- Article 164 make it obligatory for the state which possess large tribal populations to have ministers in charge of tribal affairs.
- Article 339 (2) empowers the union government to issue direction to a state as to the drawing up and execution of schemes specified in the direction to be essential for the welfare of scheduled tribes in the state.
- Article 15, 16 and 19 deal with prohibition of discrimination on ground of race, caste, religion sex or place of birth, equality of appointments in matter of public employment and protection of certain rights regarding freedom to practise any profession etc.

These enable the parliaments and state legislature to ensure equality of tribal people with the rest of the citizens of this country while legislating.

- Article 23, prohibition of traffic in human beings and begger and other similar from of forces labour.
- Article 24 prohibition of employment of children in factories etc.
- Article-243 (D) Reservation seats in Panchayats and Article 243 (T) Reservation of seats in municipal bodies for scheduled tribes. Out of these reservation seats, at least 1 / 3rd has been reserved for SC/ST women.
- Article 338 Nation commission for SC and STs.

Besides, enjoying the rights, which all citizens and minorities have, the member of the scheduled tribe have been provided with special safeguards as enshrined in various articles of the constitution.

Tribal Development States and Issues in India

For implementing the constitutional provisions and objectives, it is necessary to evolve a suitable tribal policy based on a correct approach. The policy is a general frame work, strategy is the specific programing directed to achieve the spelt – out objective. Integrated tribal development approach envisages mutilevel planning at Macrow, Meso and Micro levels. The salient features of the of the approach of Integrated Tribal Development Planning are to establish functional inter-linkages between the multi-level planning units. Let us see development status and issuer of Tribes in India.

(1) Displacement

It is estimated that owing to construction of over 1500 major irrigation projects since in independence over 16 million were displaced from their villages, of which about 40 percent belong to tribal population. The government and planners are aware of the eroding resource base of and socio-cultural heritage of tribal population through a combination of development interventions, commercial interests and lack of effective legal protection to tribal population owing to unimaginative, insensitive package of

60

relief (planning commission, 1990) still the development process continued unmindful of displacement.

"The issue raised indeed will thrill the mind of anybody. Indeed we are well aware of the situation of displacement of the indigenous people in India due to urge for conservation of biodiversity and various mega projects since 1950 to 1990 near about 2 core 13 lake indigenous people are displaced due to the above reasons" (Goutam Roy Anandabazar Patrika, 14th June, 2006).

(2) Health

Tribal people from their basic way to living remote places and shyness of mixing with community at large frequently are worst suffers of health hazards. Leprosy, skin diseases, tuberculosis, anemia and diarrhea are very common among them. The health hazards related to pregnancy and malnutrition are faced by more than 90 percent of the tribals.

(3) Education

According to United Nations Educational Scientific and Cultural Organization (2004) Female education is the best investment for reducing poverty, improving health and ensuring social well being "The educational status of tribal population is poor as indicated by literary rate of 41.5 percent as compared to All India average of 65.4 percent (2001). Further there exists disparity in tribal education between males and females since the literary rate of tribal males and females was found to be 59.2 percent and 34.8 percent respectively. The literacy rate of tribal female was found to be less than the national literary rate of females (54.2 percent) (Census of India 2001)

(4) Child Labour

According to the 61st round of National sample survey organization (NSSO 2004-2005), the child labour in India is around 9.01 million. Majoarity of the child labour participation is concentrated in rural areas. The tribal children, who represent the most impoverished population segment, are twice likely to be engaged in gainful economic activities than the rest of the children. A high incident to child labour and a low level of school participation of tribal children continue to pose serious problem of India. Despite the constitutional protection to the tribal people of India.

(5) Housing

Housing facilities being most fundamental requirement of human survival a question of identity requires attention. India in 1996, 28% of the tribals were without houses (Economic Survey 1998). The situation is even more dreadful while trails are displaced and or affected by development project of natural calamities.

(6) Safe Drinking Water and Sanitation

Inadequate sanitation, poor hyaline and lack of safe water supply result not only in more sickness and death but also in higher health costs, lower worker productivity, lower school enrolment and relention rate of girls and perhaps most importantly the denial of the right of all people to live in dignity (WHO-2011)

Nearly 80 percent out of 68.89% - 2011 in India in the rural area people do not have sanitation facilities and they defecate in the open. But more people own a mobile phone.

(7) Land Alienation problem

The tribals are losing their holding of land due to loopholes in legal provisions, due faulty implementation of Act and due to exploitation by business men and money lenders. Many primitive communities even today to not only consider land as a means of livelihood but consider it as an important element of their life. Thus the most important issue in tribal areas is their ownership on land i.e. their right on land and its holding.

(8) Public Distribution System

An increasing number of tribals have been dependent on the public distribution system since land has been unable to provide food anymore. However, the present system of targeting has often excluded them and has resulted in widespread malnutrition and starvation deaths. The search for food and fuel has proved to be more dangerous, more labourious and burdensome for women, who have to now go for and into the depth of the forests for gathering food not provided by the government.

(9) Social and Economic Condition

(1) In India 58% of the Tribal people, below poverty line with a high concentration in states like Andhra Pradesh, Rajasthan, UP, Bihar, Orissa and West Bengal.

(2) More than half (54%) of children are undernourished (Rachakrishna 2004) (3) Sixty Five percent of tribal people do not know read and write in India, tribal community woman burden double discrimination (gender and caste) (Ghanshyam, 2006)

(10) Violence and Crime

The violence one towards women and men of the tribal community includes many kind of harmful physical emotional and sexual behaviours against women and girls that are most often carried out by family members but also at times by strangers. In India, 5791 crimes were registered against tribal people (2006) in which 195 tribes were murdered and 699 tribal women were raped. It is compared with 2005 to 2006, crime against tribal people, is increased. Every 18 minutes : A crime is committed against a subalten people.

Reference

1. Amir Hasan (1992), *Tribal Development in India*, Raj Prakash Lucknow.
2. Mahesh Gamit and J.C. Patel (2013), *Tribal Development Perspectives & Issues*, Vista Publishers, Jaipur.
3. K. Padma (2011), *Globalisation Tribals & Gender*, Madhav Book, Gurgaon.
4. Ghanshyam Shah & Other (2006), *Untouchability in Rural India*, Sage Publication, New Delhi.

5. Radhakrushna Rande Ravi (2004), *Malnutrition in India : Trends and Determinants*, Economic and Political Weekly : 39 (9) PP 671-676.
6. Lal B. Suresh (2006), *Health Status and Health Practice among the tribals: A case study in A P*, Social Anthropology Vol.3 No.2, Serials Publication, New Delhi.
7. B. Suresh Lal (2014), *Tribal Development Issues in India* Vol-I, Serials Publications, New Delhi.
8. Bose, A, Tyagi RP and Sinha, IP (1990), *Demography of Tribal Development*, B.R. Publishing Corporation, New Delhi.
9. Rath Govinda Chandra (2006), *Tribal Development in India*, The Contemporary Debate, Sage Publication, New Delhi.
10. *World Health Organization* (2001), World Report-2011.

SC/ST DEVELOPMENT NEEDS
A FRESH LOOK

Prof. Shankarbhai L. Rot[1], Prof. Sangita K. Taviyad[2]

[1]*Smt. J. P. Shroff Arts College, Tithal Road, Valsad*
[2]*Art, Commerce & Computer Science College, Manavadar,*

Introduction

The Scheduled Castes (SCs) and Scheduled Tribes (STs) are the disadvantaged sections of the society due to socio-economic exploitation and isolation since a long time. The Scheduled Castes are notified in 31 States/UTs of India and Scheduled Tribes in 30 States. The number of ethnic Groups notified as Scheduled Castes & Scheduled Tribes in different States/UTs are 1241 & 705 respectively. As per the 2011 census the total population of SCs & Sts are 25.20% (SC – 16.60% and ST – 8.60%)[3] Scheduled Castes (SCs) constitute about 201.4 million representing 16.60% of the total population of India (Census 2011). The population of Scheduled Tribes (STs) is 104.3 million (Census 2011) constituting 8.6% of the total population of the country.

The Constitution of India gives the Rights to all its citizens as it is given preamble-
"......to secure to all its citizens:
JUSTICE, social, economic and political;
EQUALITY of status and of opportunity;
and to promote among them all
FRATERNITY assuring the dignity of the individual and
the unity and integrity of the Nation...."[4]

Now what is the level of achievement of these goals in terms of SCs & STs.

Scheduled Castes (SCs), since long, have been relegated to low income generating occupations, inferior

---

[3] Census of India 2011 : Release of Primary Census Abstract Data Highlight, 30th April 2013.
[4] Palekar S.A. Indian Constitution Government and Politics, Jaipur: ABD Publishers, 2003. P11

trades, unhygienic environment and menial occupations. Though un-touchability has been abolished by the Constitution, caste rigidities continues to confine many SC workers in low occupations.

STs have their own distinctive culture and are geographically isolated with low socio-economic conditions. It is well established that the central region of India, despite being resource rich, inhabits the poorest people who have not benefited from social and economic development to the same extent as people in other regions have, and in many cases have actually been harmed from displacement that growth entails.

The Provisions for Social Upliftment SCs & STs.

There are many Constitutional safeguards for the welfare, development and protection of SCs and STs in the country like Article 14 – Equal rights and Opportunities, Article 15 – Protection against discrimination on the grounds of caste, religion, race, sex etc., Article 15(4) – Advancement of Socially and educationally backward Classes, Article 16(4) – Reservation in appointments, Article 46 – Educational and Economic interests of Weaker sections, in particular to SCs/STs to protect them from social injustice and all forms of exploitation, Article 330, 332 and 335- reservation of seats in Lok Sabha, Legislative Assemblies and Services, Protection of Civil Rights (PCR) Act, 1955 & Prevention of Atrocities (POA) Act, 1989 – Protection of STs and SCs from social discrimination like untouchability, exploitation and atrocities. There are Constitutional provisions of 5th and 6th Schedule for the protection and administrative dispensation of tribals in the Central Indian States and North-Eastern Region States. The two statutory Commissions viz. National Commission for SCs and National Commission for STs have an important role in safeguarding the rights and interests of the SCs and STs.

During the first four Five Year Plans the strategy followed for the development of SCs was removal of untouchability (PCR Act, 1955), improving social status by providing them educational and economic opportunities, subsidised housing, various agricultural programmes,

Financial assistance through Finance Corporations, 20-Point Economic Programme to improve their living conditions which was mainly welfare oriented. Sixth Five Year Plan (1980-85) is the first plan which gave emphasis for the comprehensive development of SCs in terms of Special Component Plan - a new strategy with a due share of benefits in physical and financial terms from the various programmes of every sector through cluster and saturation approach. During Seventh and Eighth Five Year Plans economic development for individual families and groups of families of SCs, liberation of scavengers and provision of employment to the sanitation workers, enactment of the Prevention of Atrocities (POA) Act, 1989 promotion of Voluntary Organizations for training and mobilising community resources. The Ninth and Tenth Five Year Plans emphasised 'SCs Participation' in the development process through Panchayati Raj Institutions and the strategies adopted are Social Empowerment; Economic Empowerment; Social Justice to accelerate the on-going process of improving the socio-economic status of the SCs.

The Provisions for Economic Upliftment SCs & STs.

The Tribal Sub-Plan (TSP) strategy was evolved for the rapid socio-economic development of tribal people in the 5th Five Year Plan has the objectives of socio-economic development and Protection of STs against exploitation through legal and administrative support for narrowing the gap between their levels of development to that of the general communities.

The important aspect of this strategy is to ensure allocation of funds for TSP areas at least in proportion to the ST population of each of the State/UT. The TSP strategy is now being implemented through 196 Integrated Tribal Development Projects/Integrated Tribal Development Agencies (ITDPs/ITDAs), 259 Modified Area Development approach (MADA) Pockets, 82 Clusters and 75 Primitive Tribal Groups in 23 TSP States/UTs.

The Tribal Sub-Plan Programmes are to be financed by the following sources: (a) Tribal Sub Plan funds form

State /U.T Plans and Central Ministries/Departments, (b) Special Central Assistance (SCA) to Tribal Sub Plan (TSP), (c) Grants under Article 275 (1) of the Constitution to the States/U.Ts, (d) Funds through Central Sector Schemes, (e) Funds from Centrally Sponsored Schemes and (f) Institutional Finance.

The Special Component Plan -SCP (*recently changed to* Scheduled Caste Sub Plan) was designed to channelise the flow of benefits and outlays from the general sectors in the plan of the States/UTs and Central Ministries for the development of SCs in physical and financial terms. These plans are envisaged to help poor SC families through composite income generating programmes to cover all the major occupational groups amongst SCs such as agricultural labourers, small and marginal farmers, share-croppers, fishermen, sweepers and scavengers, urban un-organised labourers. The strategy of SCP since evolved in 1979 is aimed at: (a) Economic development through beneficiary oriented programmes for raising their income and creating assets; (b) Basti oriented schemes for infrastructure development through provision of drinking water supply, link roads, house-sites, housing etc. (c) Educational and Social development activities like establishment of primary schools, health centres, vocational centres, community halls, women work place etc. The actual flow of funds to SCP from the total State/UT. Plan becomes much lesser than what should have been as per the percentage of the population of SCs in the State/UT. Only a few Central ministries/departments are formulating SCP.

Many of the Ministries/Departments are not providing funds to SCP on the basis of population proportions on the premise that, their budget and schemes are non-divisible in nature. The allocation of SCP funds reveals that during 7th, 8th and 9th Plan were far less than the SC population percentage in the States and Central Ministries/Depts. were not allocating even the minimum amount.

Causes For Backwardness

There so many causes for backwardness of SCs/STs. Some of them are as under.

(1) *Illiteracy main cause of backwardness of SCs/STs*

Eminent sociologist TG Jogdamb said that illiteracy was the main cause of backwardness of Scheduled Castes and Scheduled Tribes in India. "Successive governments have taken several populist measures to uplift the Scheduled Castes and Tribes in the country but illiteracy remains the main cause for their backwardness"[5]

(2) *Poor governance*

Apart from poor utilisation of funds, tribals have also suffered because of the poor quality of governance. Programme delivery has deteriorated everywhere in India, but more so in tribal areas.

(3) *Poor Bargaining ability*

it is important to understand that tribal communities are vulnerable not only because they are poor, assetless and illiterate compared to the general population; often their distinct vulnerability arises from their inability to negotiate and cope with the consequences of their forced integration with the mainstream economy, society, cultural and political system, from which they were historically protected as the result of their relative isolation.

Post-independence, the requirements of planned development brought with them the spectre of dams, mines, industries and roads on tribal lands. With these came the concomitant processes of displacement, both literal and metaphorical — as tribal institutions and practices were forced into uneasy existence with or gave way to market or formal state institutions (most significantly, in the legal sphere), tribal peoples found themselves at a profound disadvantage with respect to the influx of better-equipped outsiders into tribal areas. The repercussions for the already fragile socio-economic livelihood base of the tribals were devastating —

---

[5] **DNA,** Saturday, 27 November 2010

ranging from loss of livelihoods, land alienation on a vast scale, to hereditary bondage.

(4) *Unspent budgetary balances*

The concerned ministries are not able to spend even the limited budget allotted to them for the purpose of upliftment of SCs/STs. There has been large surrender of funds by the Ministries every year.

(5) *Lack of Proper Monitoring*

Even the Planning Commission does not monitor regularly the impact of existing policies on the tribal population and pull up the concerned sectoral Ministries. There seems to be an obsession in Government of India with financial budget and not with the impact that policies (or the lack of it) have on the marginalised peoples. Policies and budgetary provisions, despite the rhetoric, have not been integrated so far. Changes in policy or laws, are not seen as an integral part of the development process because these have no direct financial implications. One lesser known reason for this isolation is that development and planning in India are associated with spending of money. That Planning *means* Expenditure, *and this will lead to* Development is the mindset behind such beliefs. The Indian planner unfortunately has still to understand the difference between planning and budgeting. This is where a systemic change is needed in India. In addition to spending budgets, we need to give equal importance to non-monetary issues such as institutions, laws, and policies.

Suggestions

The socio-economic conditions of the SCs and STs in the country shows that, though there is some improvement in literacy, drinking water availability, road connectivity and agricultural practices, employment opportunities and increase in income of SCs and STs since 1951 but, the gap between the SCs, STs and other general population in 2001 indicate huge gaps of 10 to 25% points in the socio-economic indicators. To achieve the comprehensive

70

development of the SCs and STs, the following issues need to be addressed with determined efforts.

(1) **Perspective Planning**: Perspective Planning for SCs and STs development in every State for the development of SCs and STs by setting clear objectives, resources available/requirement, outcomes and goals with periodic bench mark surveys for the regions, districts, taluka, Clusters (areas, villages) by setting realistic targets. Though some States have prepared the State and human development reports, but the social category wise data in detail is not being prepared regularly.

(2) **Allocation of proper resources**: States/U.Ts and Central Ministries/ Depts. are not allocating SC and ST population proportionate funds towards Special Component Plan and Tribal Sub Plan in their Annual Plans. The guidelines issued by the nodal Ministries of Social Justice & Empowerment, Tribal Affairs and Planning Commission regarding SCP, TSP, SCA to SCP and SCA to TSP and grants under Article 275(1) of the Constitution are not being strictly adhered. The nodal Ministries and Planning Commission need to streamline this procedure for adherence to these guidelines

(3) **Decentralised and integrated Planning and functional autonomy**: The guidelines for the decentralized district level planning, allocation of resources of at least 30% to district bodies by most of the States are yet to follow this. Integrated planning of the sectoral departments programmes and execution of common programmes at the district and project level through pooling of resources and single line administration advocated in tribal areas is not working effectively though it is in place in some States like A.P., Gujarat and Orissa. More financial and executive powers need to be given to the implementing agencies at the District/Project level functionaries with infrastructure and supporting mechanism for timely execution of projects.

(4) **Effective Monitoring mechanism:** Monitoring mechanism observed is weak in the States and is being done by the nodal Social Welfare and Tribal Welfare Departments only for their own departmental schemes and there is no proper and regular monitoring mechanism for the overall SCP and TSP programmes/ schemes and 20 point programme at the State, District, Block and Village level. The ITDPs/ITDAs in the selected States review meetings are irregular and routine in nature. Tribal Advisory Committee (TAC) meetings in Scheduled Area States which are mandatory are not regular. The State Governor's report are not filed regularly. Monitoring Committees at the State, District and Block level need to be established and functionally operative. Every State need to have now Social Audit Programme with the involvement of elected representatives, beneficiaries and credited VOs/NGOs on the completed programmes/schemes.

(5) **Personnel posting in tribal/ scheduled areas and Scheduled Caste areas:** Deployment of efficient and young officers at the ITDP/ITDA and SC concentrated Districts need to be ensured for the effective implementation of SCP and TSP programmes with proper incentives/disincentives for the posting and functional efficiency for the success of the strategies and schemes.

(6) **The role of nodal Ministries and Planning Commission:** The nodal Ministries of Social Justice & Empowerment and Tribal Affairs have issued guidelines for SCA to SCP, SCA to TSP and Article 275 (1) of the Constitution besides operating many of the CS and CSS schemes which need to be implemented effectively through timely and proper releases, monitoring by periodic field visits, calling of reports and conducting evaluation. As Special Central Assistance is linked to SCP and TSP implementation process in the States the nodal Ministries should use it as leverage for streamlining and effective implementation. Planning Commission has issued

guidelines and directives to States/U.Ts on several occasions and these needs to be strictly enforced through their Annual Plan review meetings. The Central Tri-Partite Committee need to play an important role with the involvement of nodal Ministries and SC/ST Commissions for the effective implementation of SCP and TSP in the States/U.Ts and Central Ministries/Depts.

(7) **The role of NGOs**: NGOs are involved in most of the states in STs and SCs development activities. Their role in each State need to be charted out by the State to supplement the efforts of the state administration keeping in view the recently announced National Policy of Voluntary Sector to increase the Civil Society role. Their involvement in the Social Audit and effective monitoring of Government programmes also should be encouraged. However, the credentials of VOs/NGOs and their activities need also to be ascertained before giving them responsibility

(8) **Schemes/programmes funds to be realistic in ST and SC areas**: Most of the State and Central Schemes are designed as general schemes and they are also being implemented in ST and SC concentrated interior and isolated areas which need flexibility, different norms and standards for its success.

(9) **Identification of beneficiaries**: As most of the socio-economic schemes under SCP and TSP are targeting BPL families, the listing and identification of the beneficiaries need to be more transparent, which needs regular up-gradation for implementation and monitoring. Regular surveys, identification of eligible beneficiaries and involving the Panchayats/Gram Sabha, Block/District Panchayats, wide publicity/Media/Websites will ensure transparency.

(10) **State Finance Corporations need to be revitalized**: Most of the State Governments are implementing their State poverty alleviation and economic development programmes through their SC/ST Finance Development Corporations which are also working as State Channelising agencies of the National SC/ST/Safai Karmacharies Finance and Development

Corporations. Though they are in existence for the last 30 years, they are yet to make a serious dent for the entrepreneurship/skill/ economic development of the SC/ST beneficiaries which need to be geared up in terms of its financial, human resource management and coverage of beneficiaries. Some States like T.N and Haryana SC Finance Corporations are doing well and have innovative agriculture, irrigation and land purchase and development schemes which need to be emulated by other States.

(11) **Atrocities and discrimination laws and stringent punishment**: One of the basic objectives of SCP and TSP is the protection of SCs and STs against all types of exploitation and discrimination. However, it is observed that, the PCR and POA act though in place still the atrocities and discrimination are reported and in some States increasing. These laws need to be stringent and the 20 point programme which has a component of welfare and security needs monitoring regularly at the Chief Minister level as being done in some States like Chhattisgarh and Tamil Nadu States now.

(12) **Involvement of local bodies**: The planning of bottom-up approach envisaged of Village-Block-District –State is not happening though it has been attempted in States like Kerala, Gujarat and Maharashtra. Similarly the PESA Act, 1996 in Scheduled Areas, empowering the Gram Sabha with powers in resource management and decision making is not in place and they are really defunct bodies due to State Govts. apathy for this. The laws enacted for the rights and protection of the SCs/STs like Forests Right Act, Resettlement & Rehabilitation policy, Excise policy, Money Lenders Act etc. though in place but still large scale land alienation, displacement, money lending, exploitation, discrimination, atrocities are increasing particularly in tribal areas which needs strict enforcement of laws and involvement of local bodies, beneficiaries/affected persons, NGOs/VOs in their proper implementation.

(13) **Implementation of recommendations, laws, acts and policies**: There are large body of data, task force reports, special Committees reports, SC and ST Commission Reports, Planning Commission Working Groups and Steering Committees reports, Circulars and the Guidelines, Policies, Laws, Acts and Constitutional provisions but in spite of this the ground reality is that, these exists in the government departments and there is a need to translate them into action by the decision makers and political authority at the State and Centre for the welfare and development of SCs and STs in the country.

(14) **A systemic change is needed**: It is unfortunate that MOTA does not give sufficient attention to the important problems of the tribals on the plea that many of these subjects, such as land alienation, displacement, FRA and PESA, have not been allotted to it. Even then the Ministry should play a more activist role in addressing these issues by pursuing with the concerned Ministries, where these subjects get a low importance, as the Ministries' excuse is that they are concerned with 'bigger' and more 'general' issues. At least, MOTA can set up a monitoring mechanism to bring out the dismal picture of tribal areas that would put pressure on the sectoral Ministries and the states to improve their policies and implementation. MOTA would be taken seriously by other Ministries only if it does evidence based advocacy by analysing why delivery in the forest regions is not improving.

As tribal people in India perilously, sometimes hopelessly, grapple with these tragic consequences, the small clutch of bureaucratic programmes have done little to assist the precipitous pauperisation, exploitation and disintegration of these communities. Tribal people respond occasionally with anger and assertion, but often also in anomie and despair, because the following persistent problems have by and large remained unattended to:

- Land alienation
- Indebtedness

- Relation with forests, and government monopoly over MFPs, and non-implementation of the Forest Rights Act, 2006
- Ineffective implementation of Panchayats (Extension to the Scheduled Areas) Act of 1996 (PESA, 1996) for Schedule V areas.
- Involuntary displacement due to development projects and lack of proper rehabilitation.
- Poor utilisation of government funds, and
- Poor delivery of government programmes

These issues needing urgent attention are under the jurisdiction of Ministries of Environment & Forests, Rural Development, Panchayati Raj, etc., where they do not get adequate attention. The present approach of the Ministry of Tribal Affairs (MOTA) is to confine its attention to its own budget and the schemes that are under its control, such as grants to NGOs, scholarships. It is unfortunate that MOTA does not put any pressure on other Ministries, who have been vested with the responsibility to ensure that basic justice and development reaches them. MOTA does not even monitor whether the basic services in education, health, or nutrition are reaching the tribal hamlets.

References

Bijoy C. R. Policy brief on Panchayat Raj (Extension to Scheduled Areas) Act of 1996, New Delhi: UNDP, 2012

Chandramouli C. (Dr.). Census of India 2011 Release of Primary Census Abstract Data Highlight, New Delhi: REGISTRAR GENERAL & CENSUS COMMISSIONER, INDIA, 30TH APRIL 2013

Information Technology Section (ITS). DPI Press Kit. *New york:United Nations Department of Public Information, 1997*

Ministry of *Tribal* Affairs. Draft National Policy on Tribals: Suggestions for Improvement. New Delhi: Press Information Bureau, GOI, 2006

Prasad Neeta. Yojana, vol 55, New Delhi : Publications Division, GOI, April 2011

Sachar Rajindar. Social, Economic and Educational Status of the Muslim Community of India A Report. New Delhi: Publications Division, GOI, 2006

Socio Economic and Educational Development Society (SEEDS). Research Study on Livelihood Options Assets Creation out of Special Component Plan (SCP) & Tribal Sub Plan (TSP) Schemes and its Impact among SCs and STs in India. New Delhi: Planning Commission, Government of India, 2007

A GLANCE AT MAJOR PROBLEMS OF WEAKER SECTORS OF DEMOCRATIC INDIA

Dr. Minakshiben C. Vania
Assistant Professor
R.P.Anada College of Education, Borsad

Span of 67 years is not less. Yes, after 67 years of independent India we are facing problems in fulfilling some basic needs of the people of world's one of the largest democratic country i.e. India. We can't deny the bitter fact that we have failed to achieve the Indian constitutional goal of equality and justice. 'Five year plans' were developed, executed and monitored for development and wellbeing of people by providing good infrastructure to bloom in the global market. But the present scenario shows the different picture of social and economical development. Indeed the impact of globalization has been highly positive on most sphere of economic and social life. The process of globalization has helped Indian economy to grow rapidly in last decade. Foreign countries have substantially increased their investments in Indian companies. Wages of Indian labor has been increased. Several new types of industries have come up. As a result we find an overall happy picture but forget to see the dark side of progressive, vibrant and virtually internationally competitive India. If try to see through MAKE INDIA or PMEGP, we may understand the clear picture of Indian economy. Indian bazaar is filled with China products. The import of electric goods is at second rank. Home made products are more costly then imported products due to less subsidy, high rate of interest, electricity and inadequate transport facility. These are the basic problems we have to fight for.

According to Planning Commission (Year 2011-12) the ratio below Poverty Line is as below.

Rural sector 25.7% Urban sector 12.7%   All India 21.9%

The above ratio shows the seriousness of Indian society.

Slogans like "EK SAKSHAR EK NIRAKSHAR BHANAVE", "SAVE GIRL CHILD", and "WOMEN EMPOWERMENT or EK KADAM SWACHCHH BHAR KI AUR" points out the loop holes of the policy and ill implementation of requisite work of five year plans. To assess the political, social cultural and economical condition of the nation, we must have a glance at weaker sections.

Weaker sectors of democratic India

The major weaker sectors or the problems of the main sectors can be listed as below.

- Education
- Health and hygiene
- Women empowerment
- Agricultural field
- Small and rural entrepreneur
- Transportation

Limitations of Education Field

The nation known for its Nalanda, Taxsheela and ValbhiVidyapith is nowhere in the race of top ten university. The main reason is 'rattamaro pass ho jao' examination system. Leakage of question papers and answer sheet scams shows the failure of examination system. Concept of open book examination and semester system has been proven failure. This happen perhaps because the system design of developed countries was applied without properly reviewed in Indian context. Our classroom climate is not so as the developed countries. The rate of passing in various competitive exams like I.A.S. C.A. UGC CAT NET TOEFEL or even TAT or TET indicates that something wrong is prevailing in the education system. Due to number of self financed colleges literate unemployment ratio has been increased and higher education has become more expensive. No wonder as a side effect of self finance colleges will widen the gap of two classes, poor and prosperous. The structure of entrance test and job examinations lead the youth towards race for knowledge (information) instead of reaching at depth of syllabus and cultivating values, skills and attitude.

To overcome these problems the ratio of student teachers should be maintained strictly. Overcrowded classroom especially at primary level must be seized. Examination system, syllabus and semester system policy needs to be revised in Indian context. Open book exam with due respect under expertise supervision need to bring back. Career development programme, guidance and admission in student's interesting fields through various personality tests should be promoted.

Health and Hygiene

The eleventh plan was targeted to ensure electricity connection and clean drinking water. Generally Panchayat and Nigam manage and provide facility of health, hygiene and cleanliness. Looking around us, we find scarcity of clean surroundings. Improper drainage and garbage distortion system is the main cause of diseases. According to one survey only 31.7% of families in rural area and 82.5% of families in urban area have proper drainage facility, whereas 32% in villages and 75.8% in urban areas family have garbage disposure facility.

Swachchha Bharat Abhiyan is indeed a good step taken. But along with this the vacant posts for the cleaning staff should be filled. Attitude for cleanliness must be developed in children and youth through education and multi media. Strict rules must be made and implemented.

Women Empowerment

Today we find women in every field. But the ratio is not much pleasing. The number of enrollment in social and service sectors like teaching profession or medical field has seen largein number but enrollment and job of female student in engineering, architect and entrepreneur field is very low.

The participation in Directory board of BSE 100companies is indicated below.

1. Total Directors 1,112 out of that 59 female Directors = 5.30%
2. Executive Directors 323 out of that 8 female EXE. Directors = 2.5%
3. Non Executive Directors 789 out of that 51female EXE. Directors = 6.5%

Awareness for women empowerment must be spread. The attitude towards boys and girls should be balanced and the bringing up of children should be neutral. The society where respect for women is seen, found to be prosperous. The crime doesn't cease by lows but understanding makes the difference. Promotion of Education for girls in every field must be enhanced and motivated. The lady acquiring status in various fields must be appreciated and all the girls must be made aware of their rights and given proper information how they can achieve their carrier in the fields where man's monopoly is counted.

Limitations of Agricultural Field

The progress of agriculture sector has been reduced due to encouragement to urbanization and industrialization. Population burst is another problem. The ratio of land per head in India in context of the world is 0.09: 4.5. Beside this other major delimitations are as follows.

➤ Indian agriculture system is failed in planning beneficial insurance plans for farmers on crop failure. Till now only 14% of farmers have taken advantage of crop insurance policy (Pak Suraksha Yojana). Maximum benefit is taken by big rich farmers.
➤ Indian agriculture system is dependent on natural rain water. Though Major part (60%) of Indian society belongs to rural and farming the Irrigation system is inadequate at world level.
➤ Due to fewer subsidies to agriculture, lack of knowledge about loan facility, low price of farming product at grass root level and expense on seed, manure and irrigation the Indian farmer overlapped

under debts. 22000 cases of farmer's suicide have been registered till now.

➤ Due to dual policy of world trade organization India has only 1% proportion of agricultural export where as this ratio is of 44% of developed country.

➤ New trends, technology and modern tools of agriculture is not yet accepted by traditional orthodox very small scale farmers of Indian society. Still they work at traditional old method of farming in many parts of the country.

➤ As a solution of above problems the Indian farmers trend to sell the agricultural land to housing or industrial sectors.

➤ Out of all agricultural land 62% of land is acquired by 10% of farmers while 39% of land is acquired by all other 90% of farmers. This shows the imbalance among land owners, rich farmers, poor farmers and farm laborers.

Use of improved seeds and fertilizers along with proper irrigation facilities can make multiple cropping and enhance productivity. Though the ration of production is increased due to lack of direct selling farmers doesn't get its benefits. Clutches of Agents lead to low prize of buying from farmers. Credit co operative sectors should be strengthening for the benefits of small farmers.

Need of more Micro, Small and Rural Entrepreneur

During the period of 1950-51 our economy was depended on agricultural sectors. In present era compare to agriculture sector industrial sector seems more power on economy. Globalization and liberalization has bad impact on these small scale industries. Micro, Small and Medium Enterprises (MSME) contribute nearly 8 percent of the country's GDP, 45 percent of the manufacturing output and 40 percent of the exports. They provide the largest share of employment after agriculture. They are the nurseries for entrepreneurship and innovation. They are widely dispersed across the country and produce a diverse range of products and services to meet the needs of the local markets, the global market and the national and international value chains., In article "Role of small scale industries in Indian economy" shrinivasulaBayine(August 2004) compared small scale industries as a backbone of our economy. It indicates that this sector contributes enormously to the socio-economic development of the country and play crucial role in providing large employment opportunities at comparatively lower capital cost than large industries and also help in industrialization of rural & backward areas. According to one survey, capital investment of one crore rupees in small scale industry generate employment of about 300 persons where as large and medium industry provide employment to only 30 people on the same amount. Large industry leads the society towards capitalization. So in order toreduce regional imbalances, assuring more equitable distribution of national income and wealth MSMEs are complementary to large industries as ancillary units.

A step taken by the government for development of small scale industry is IMEGP(Prime Minister Employment Generation Programme) The detail is given at the end of this paper.

Transportation

The facility of public transportation seems very weak. Especially the routes of public ST buses are decreased. The budget sanctioned for buying new ST buses is not yet utilized. The places of bus stations, roads and the condition of local route buses compiles middle class people, to use private vehicles to commute at their work places causes unnecessary fuel wastage and increases pollution.

To increase the route and frequency for public transport is the solution for most problems of this sector.

Conclusion

India has to fight the battle of burning problems at three fronts in order to be a politically and economically leading country. First is to provide adequate infrastructure and sufficient subsidy to rural small scale industry. Second is to increase demand of homemade product (Made in India) and maintain quality at lower cost. And third but the main important is to plan human resource through proper admission on basis of aptitude test and emphasizing development of skills and values instead of merely information and 'Gokhanpatti". Above all awareness among people, patriotism and attitude will make the future of India bright.

References

Dr. SrinivasulaBayine (August 2004) The Role and Performance of SSI in IndianEconomy. The ICFSAI Journal of managementerial Economics. The ICFAI School of Economics, the ICFAI University of Hyderabad.

ArthSankalangujarati magazine of Economics and Commerce ISSN 0976-2086

http://www.daldrup.org/University/International%20Management/Globalization%20in%20India.pdf

ANNEXURE – I

Scheme for providing financial assistance to set up new enterprises under PMEGP	
Related Scheme	Prime Minister Employment Generation Programme (PMEGP)
Description	The Scheme is implemented by Khadi and Village Industries Commission (KVIC), as the nodal agency at the National level. At the State level, the Scheme is implemented through State KVIC Directorates, State Khadi and Village Industries Boards (KVIBs) and District Industries Centres (DICs) and banks. The Government subsidy under the Scheme is routed by KVIC through the identified Banks for eventual distribution to the beneficiaries / entrepreneurs in their Bank accounts.
Nature of assistance	The maximum cost of the project/unit admissible under manufacturing sector is Rs.25 lakh and under business/service sector is Rs.10 lakh. Levels of funding under PMEGP

Categories of beneficiaries under PMEGP	Beneficiary's contribution (of project cost)	Rate of Subsidy (of project cost)	
Area (location of project/unit)		Urban	Rural
General Category	10%	15%	25%
Special (including SC / ST / OBC / Minorities / Women, Ex-servicemen, Physically handicapped, NER, Hill and Border areas, etc.	05%	25%	35%
The balance amount of the total project cost will be provided by Banks as term loan as well as working capital.			

Who can apply?	Any individual, above 18 years of age. At least VIII standard pass for projects costing above Rs.10 lakh in the manufacturing sector and above Rs. 5 lakh in the business / service sector. Only new projects are considered for sanction under PMEGP. Self Help Groups (including those belonging to BPL provided that they have not availed benefits under any other Scheme), Institutions registered under Societies Registration Act,1860; Production Co-operative Societies, and Charitable Trusts are also eligible. Existing Units (under PMRY, REGP or any other scheme of Government of India or State Government) and the units that have already availed Government Subsidy under any other scheme of Government of India or State Government are NOT eligible.
How to apply?	The State/Divisional Directors of KVIC in consultation with KVIB and Director of Industries of respective states (for DICs) will give advertisements locally through print & electronic media inviting applications along with project proposals from prospective beneficiaries desirous of establishing the enterprise/ starting of service units under PMEGP. The beneficiaries can also submit their application online at http://www.kviconline.gov.in/pmegp/pmegponlineapp and take the printout of the application and submit the same to respective offices along with Detailed Project Report and other required documents.

GLOBALIZATION AND SCHEDULE CASTE

Dr. Kamalnayan B. Parmar[1], Dr. Hiralkumar M. Barot[2]

[1]*Assoc. Prof. Shree R P Anada College of Education, Borsad.*
[2]*Asst. Prof., Sheth MNC College of Education, Dabhoi.*

Introduction

Globalization is the new buzzword that has come to dominate the world since the nineties of the Last centuries. It is the most widely debated and discussed phenomenon in all over the world. It is based on the principle of unrestrained functioning of the free market economy. In the paradigm of globalization, state is reduced into a sort of security mechanism to protect its citizens from internal disruption and external threats. State is not supposed to care for social and economic Interests of its citizens. The world opinion is divided on what constitutes globalization and whether globalization is good or bad. The fact is that today almost every nation state is forced to become a part of a global economy.

Globalization as a new world economic order imposed on the world with a promise of more prosperity, progress and freedom for all. On the contrary, evidences show that globalization affected negatively in all these aspects for some communities particularly the dalit communities. (Dalits are a group of people who faced social discrimination in the worst form i.e. untouchability. It is used to connote the untouchables known as avarnas, pariahas, out-castes, exterior-castes etc. In the present work it has been also used to connote the Scheduled Castes). More than two decades of implementation of these policies pertaining to globalization have severely affected the welfare and development of dalits. In this paper we will try to examine the magnitude and direction of the impact of these policies on the dalits in India.

Scheduled Castes

Few societies have condemned one of their sections to physical segregation as the Hindu society has done in the case of the former untouchables. The mere physical touch of an untouchable was a sin, an abomination. The segregation of a section of the Hindus as untouchables, precluded from such elementary rights as entry to public temples or the use of public wells and tanks, and whose physical touch contaminated a member of higher castes, constituted a most inhuman form of social oppression. The untouchables were the outcastes of Hindu society. Hallowed with tradition and sanctified by religion, the unsociability continued to exist in all its barbarous vigor for centuries. After independence, in 1950, the Constitution of India abolished untouchability (Article 17) and in 1955, the Parliament passed the Untouchability Offences Act. The national movement had created an atmosphere sympathetic towards the untouchables. It made it possible for the Government to provide protective discrimination in an attempt to pull out the untouchables from traditional segregation. Among the multitude of difficult tasks facing the new nation of India in 1947, none was more challenging than The integration of the most deprived 15 percent of its population-the untouchables-into unequal partnership in the emerging modern republic. Since the Govt.of India Act 1935, the untouchables became known as the Scheduled Castes. But even though untouchability and discrimination on the basis of caste are constitutionally outlawed, despite the constitutional legal support and also efforts by various voluntary agencies, it is commonly observed that they continue to be deprived of their rightful place in society. And upper castes have generally denied equal treatment to the Scheduled Castes.

The backwardness of the Scheduled castes will be evident from their unemployment, dependence on agriculture, illiteracy and social segregation. In terms of residence, housing and health conditions, the condition of the Scheduled Castes is precarious. Even now in many villages they have to suffer residential segregation and direct and indirect social boycott. There are many among them who are too poor to build their houses. On account of their poverty and unhygienic living conditions, they, in large numbers, suffer from malnutrition, physical disabilities and diseases such as tuberculosis, leprosy, malaria, and general diseases.

This is not to say that post-independence period has not brought any socioeconomic and political change in the life of the Scheduled Castes. Constitutional provisions, political process since independence and the impact of leadership of Dr. B.R.Ambedkar have created a wave of rising expectations in the life of Scheduled Castes in general and in the life of the neo-Buddhists in particular. Gradually, since then, the Scheduled Castes are slowly becoming aware of their rightful place in society and are asserting for the reordering of society for their betterment and advancement. This has created a number of pressures and pulls resulting in socio-political tensions in Indian society. Renaming Marathwada University agitation after Dr. Ambedkar was one such occasion.

Following points may be considered for the development of Scheduled Castes in an era of globalization.

1. Need of Political Education
We have accepted a democratic form of government in an un-democratic society. It is, therefore, necessary to give political education to the people about the need and genesis of welfare policies for the weaker sections.

Political education means education about nature, working and the functions of a political system in which you live. This was the duty of the elites and the leaders in the political process. Unfortunately both have miserably failed in their tasks. As a result of it, there is a lack of understanding about the problems of weaker sections which results in social tensions.

2. Lack of political will
There is a lack of political will regarding the development of Scheduled Castes. There is increasing

populism to fetch the votes of Schedules Castes and very few sincere efforts for their development. Many a times the political process has divided the Scheduled Castes. It is observed that the welfare schemes remain on paper but because of the policies there is a backlash among the upper castes.

3. Challenge of Globalization

Infact it is a high time that the leaders in the political process and academicians give a serious thought to the consequences of Liberalization, Privatization and particularly Globalization. On the lines of the Scheduled Castes. In globalization the old concepts like nationalism, sovereignty are gradually waning and the there is an erosion of a nation-state. Samuel Huntington argues that now the culture would be an important variable in international politics and not the concepts like nationalism or sovereignty. There is increasing international interdependence on the one hand giving rise to internationalism. On the other hand, the narrow and parochial loyalties are playing significant role. How to reconcile this contradiction? Here we need long term as well as short-term policies and avoid adhocism, opportunism and populism. As we have seen above globalization needs quality and the quality assumes acquiring various skills necessary for individual and social development. Because of changing nature of economy and social conditions now there are new needs, which have arisen in society, now new sections have come up in society and they have non-traditional needs. They include the needs of senior citizens, the employed married couples in metropolitan cities, and the demand for crèche is on increase. Multiplexes, food malls, shopping malls, etc have changes the life style of the middle class. In this way new needs can be found out and an attempt can be made to give response to these demands by way of providing service to them. The 21st century is a century of multi- skills and a person having more than one skill will have definitely a bright future.

4. Demand for change in the Education System

Dr. Ambedkar gave a message—"educates, agitates and organizes." But what kind of education? Present education is fast becoming irrelevant to the changing needs. It is to be understood that the present education system is the product of the colonial rule and the post-independence period Globalization and Scheduled Castes governments have done very little to change the same. In addition to increasing educational opportunities, our demand should be to make the education system more meaningful and more relevant to the changing needs in society. It may be remembered in a way, that present unemployment is mostly false one. It is unemployment of the unskilled people. Therefore an attempt is to be made to improve the quality of the people. It can be achieved by way of acquiring knowledge, skills and attitudes in the changing context. Globalization has posed a challenge to all and more to the Scheduled Castes. Unless such efforts are done the values in the constitution would not be materialized.

Reference

• Desai, A.R. (1966): Social Background of Indian Nationalism, Popular Prakashan, Bombay, (4th ed),p.263.
• Johnson, Glen, and Sipra Bose(1978): Social Mobility Among Untouchables, in Cohesion and conflict In Modern India, Vikas, New Delhi, pp. 60-61.
• Karade Jagan,(2008): Development of SC and ST in India, Cambridge scholar publishing, P 10.
• Kakade, S.R. (1990): Scheduled Castes and National Integration, Radiant publishers, New Delhi, p 2.
• Kakade, S.R.(1993): Political Attitudes Of Neo-Buddhists in Western Maharashtra, post-doctoral research funded by ICSSR, New Delhi.
• Sachchidanand(1977):The Harijan Elite, Thompson Press, Faridabad, p. 162 .

LEGAL AID AND GOVERNMENT POLICIES TO EMPOWER & SAFEGUARD THE INTERESTS OF WEAKER SECTIONS.

Jitendra Govardhanbhai Lalvani
Lecturer, Department of Social Work
Sardar Patel University, Vallabh Vidyanagar

ABSTRACT

As is commonly said that a welfare state takes care of its citizen, a welfare state believes that economic growth does not mean concentration of economic benefits in the hands of a few persons in the society but should aim at common good. Untouchables have faced all kinds of humiliation at the hands of upper varnas, the weaker sections women, children, labourers, disabled's and aged persons are facing number of problems in the Indian society. Thus a welfare state ensures that economic growth must not be achieved at the cost of the interest and welfare of weaker sections. In Indian Constitution social and economic justice finds its mention in the preamble, runs like a golden tread through Chapter III of fundamental rights and is more explicit laid down in Chapter IV of Directive Principles of State Policy. Commissions for SC and ST, women and children, Labour, Human Right are some of the agencies which can protect the weaker sections, and provide social, economic and political justice for all round development of weaker sections. At present under the mask of Liberalization, Privatization and Globalization the Welfare State simple escaping from its responsibility to protection of weaker sections, all the welfare schemes left by the State and privatized the public sector establishments. The present research paper discussed the various protections to the weaker sections particularly constitution provisions and Legislative protections and effect globalization on Indian society.

INTRODUCTION

The people of India have had a continuous civilization since 2500 BC, when the inhabitants of the Indus River valley developed an urban culture based on commerce and sustained by agricultural trade. This civilization declined around 1500 BC, probably due to ecological changes. During the second millennium BC, pastoral, Aryan-speaking tribes migrated from the northwest into the subcontinent. As they settled in the middle Ganges River valley, they adapted to antecedent cultures.

Indian people divided into four "Varnas" and above 6500 castes, man birth decided his social status. They lived in caste based professions and also suppressed in their social status. In this system majority people are far away from being educated, having property, human dignity and also they have low economic and political status. This type of system continued for a long period which resulted majority people to turn as depressed classes.

At the time of India got independence in 1947, major population was landless, illiterate, and poor livelihood. India adopted the Democratic form of government. The Constituent Assembly debates recognized that a section of people in Indian Society had been denied certain basic rights since ancient times and therefore remained economically, socially and educationally backward. As a result, this had created widespread disparities among various groups. This scenario of disparities leads to a situation that needs special measures to uplift the status of the marginalized and depressed groups.

Special provisions have also been made for the Scheduled Castes and Scheduled Tribes and other backward classes in the Constitution. The Constitution provides for protection and promotion of their social, economic, educational, cultural and political interests to remove the disparities and to bring them on par with other sections of the society. In addition, many articles in Parts III, IV, IX, IX-A, Fifth and Sixth Schedule of the Constitution reinforce these arrangements. It is an accepted fact that there is a large proportion of population which lacks land resources and suffers from deprivation of different kinds including unemployment, illiteracy and ill-health. The deprivation is more pronounced in the case of weaker sections such as women, scheduled castes, scheduled tribes, and backward communities.

Constitutional Provisions for Protection of Weaker Sections

Constitutional makers provided the different safeguard in the Constitution of India to these depressed classes. They are:

Article 14 provides that States shall not deny any person equality before law or the equal protection of laws within the territory of India. Article 15 operationalizes the concept of equality in a manner which specifically touches upon the conditions of the Scheduled Castes, Scheduled Tribes and other backward classes.

Article 38 State to secure a social order for the promotion of welfare of the people: The State shall strive to promote the welfare of the people by securing and protecting as effectively as it may a social order in which justice, social, economic and political, shall inform all the institutions of the national life. The State shall, in particular, strive to minimize the inequalities in income, and endeavour to eliminate inequalities in status, facilities and opportunities, not only amongst individuals but also amongst groups of people residing in different areas or engaged in different vocations.

Article 39 Certain principles of policy to be followed Article by the State

The State shall, in particular, direct its policy towards securing-
1. that the citizen, men and women equally, have the right to an adequate means of livelihood;
2. that the ownership and control of the material resource of the community are so distributed as best to sub-serve the common good;

3. that the operation of the economic system does not result in the concentration of wealth and means of production to the common detriment;

4. that there is equal pay for equal work for both men and women;

5. that the health and strength of workers, men and women, and the tender age of children are not abused and that citizens are not forced by economic necessity to enter avocations unsuited to their age or strength;

6. that children are given opportunities and facilities to develop in a healthy manner and in conditions of the freedom and dignity and that childhood and youth are protected against exploitation and against moral and material abandonment.

Article 39 (A) Equal Justice and free legal aid: The State shall secure that the operation of the legal system promotes justice, on a basis of equal opportunity, and shall, in particular, provide free legal aid, by suitable legislation or schemes or in any other way, to ensure that opportunities for securing justice are not denied to any citizen by reason of economic or other disabilities.

Article 46 under the Directive Principles of State Policy provides that "The State shall promote with special care, the educational and economic interest of weaker sections of the people and particular of Scheduled Castes and Scheduled Tribes and shall protect them social injustice and all forms of exploitation".

Article 366(24) defines Scheduled Castes and Article 34 identifies the process through which such groups will be identified. Similar provisions have been made for Scheduled Tribes in Article 366(25) and Article 342 respectively.

Social safeguards are contained in Article 17, 23, 24 and 25(2)(b) of the constitution. As per Article 17, untouchability is abolished and its practice in any form is forbidden. The enforcement of any disability arising out of "untouchability has been made an offence punishable in accordance with the law." Two important legislations have been enacted to give effect to contents of this Article. The Protection of Civil Rights Act, 1955 has been enacted with the objective of providing punishment for preaching and practice of untouchability, in the enforcement of any disability arising there from and for matters connected therewith.

Article 24 provides that no child below the age of 14 years shall be employed to work in any factory or mine or engaged in any hazardous employment. There are central and State Laws to prevent child labour practices and providing relief to those engaged as child labour. The Central law is The Child Labour (Prohibition and Regulation) Act, 1986. A large number of child labourers engaged in hazardous employment belong to Scheduled Castes and Scheduled Tribes.

Other Safeguards to Weaker Sections
Economic Safeguards

The provisions of Articles 23, 24 and 46 from part of economic safeguards for Scheduled Castes and the Scheduled Tribes. Article 46 provides that State shall promote with special care the educational and economic interests of weaker sections of the people and, in particular, Scheduled Castes/Scheduled Tribes and shall protect them from social injustice and all forms of exploitation. It is in pursuance of this Article that special programmes for extending educational opportunities to Scheduled Cates and Scheduled Tribes have been taken up. Institutional arrangements for their development, including earmarking of specific percentage of funds from the budget for various development activities in form of a special Component Plan for Scheduled Castes and the Scheduled Tribes sub-plan for Scheduled Tribes have also been in operation for a long time.

Educational and Cultural Safeguards

Article 15(4) empowers the State to make special provisions for advancement of any socially and economically backward classes or citizens and for Scheduled Castes and the Scheduled Tribes. This provision has enabled the State to reserve seats for Scheduled Castes and the Scheduled Tribes in educational institutions including technical, engineering and medical colleges.

Article 29(1) provides that "Any section of the citizens residing in the territory of India or any part thereof, having a distinct language, script or culture of its own shall have the right to conserve the same" Article 350(a) provides for adequate facilities for instructions in the mother tongue at the primary stage of education for children belonging to linguistic minority groups. The above Article has relevance for Scheduled Tribes as some of them have a distinct language/dialect.

Political Safeguards

Article 164(1) provides that in the specific States there shall be a Minister in charge of tribal welfare who may, in addition be in charge of welfare of Scheduled Castes, Backward Classes or any other work. Article 330 provides for reservation of seats for Scheduled Castes and the Scheduled Tribes in Lok Sabha.

Under Article 243(D), reservation of seats in Village Panchayats, Zilla Parishads has been made for Scheduled Castes and the Scheduled Tribes in proportion to their population at respective level in direct election. It has also been provided that the reserved seats for Scheduled Castes and the Scheduled Tribes shall be allotted by rotation to different constituencies in Panchayat at each level. Under Article 243-T, reservation of seats for Scheduled Castes and the Scheduled Tribes in proportion to their population has been made in municipal bodies at each level. Out of these reserved seats Scheduled Castes and the Scheduled Tribes, at least 1/3rd has been reserved for SC/ST women.

Service Safeguards

Article 16, which provides equality of opportunity for all citizens in matters relating to employment or appointment to any office under the State and prohibits any discrimination on grounds of religion, race, caste, sex, decent, place of birth, residence or any or all of them, has made a very special provision which permits Parliament to make any provision for reservation of appointments or posts in favour of any backward class of citizens which, in the opinion of the State, in not adequately represented in the services under the State. It is through this provision that reservations in appointments and promotions for Scheduled Castes and the Scheduled Tribes and for OBCs in the matter of recruitment have been made.

Article 16(4)(a), this benefits of reservation in the matter of promotion has been extended to Scheduled Castes and the Scheduled Tribes to overrule the judgment of the Supreme Court. Article 16(4)(b) has further made provisions to permit backlog vacancies as a separate category in any year for determining the ceiling of 50% reservation on total number of vacancies that year.

Article 335 provides that the reservation provisions shall be made taking into consideration efficiency of administration. Through a specific amendment to the Constitution, the State has been empowered to make any relaxation for qualifying mark in any examination or lowering the standards of evaluation for enforcing reservation in matters of promotion to any class or classes of service or posts in connection with the affairs of the Union or of the State. In addition to the protections referred to above, which deal with both Scheduled Castes and the Scheduled Tribes, special safeguards have also been made for Scheduled Tribes.

Article 244 provides for legislation for special problems for Scheduled areas and lays down provisions of the 5th schedule in respect of administration and control of such Social Justice the legal instruments areas. Provisions also been made for administration of tribal areas in the 6th Schedule. 5th Schedule to the Constitution, under Article 244(1) authorizes the Governor to direct that a particular law or notification passed by Parliament or Legislative Assembly shall not apply to the Scheduled area or any part thereof or shall apply subject to certain exceptions and modifications. Governor is also authorized to make regulation for peace and good government in the Scheduled areas of the State.

Article 275(1) provides that specific allocations may be made from the Consolidated Funds of India to give as grant-in aid for each such area for meeting the cost of schemes of development and for promoting the welfare of Scheduled Tribes in the State. Similar provision exits for such special grants for the 6th Scheduled area.

Article 338 of the Constitution provides for a National Commission for Scheduled Castes and the Scheduled Tribes and specifies the functions it would discharge and the report it is required to present to the President.

Enforcing Equality and Removing Disability Untouchability Offences Act, 1955

Through Article 17 of the Constitution, untouchability was abolished and its practice in any form had been abolished. Untouchability means the practices evolved as social restrictions in sharing food, access to public places, offering prayers and performing religious services, entry in temple and other public places and denial of access to drinking water sources, etc. Within 5 years of adoption of Constitution of India, the Untouchability (Offences) Act, 1955 was enacted by Parliament. The Act contained a significant provision that where any of the forbidden practices "is committed in relation to member of Scheduled Caste" the Court shall presume, unless the contrary is proved, that such act was committed on the ground of Untouchability. This implied that the burden of the proof lies on the accused and not on the prosecution.

Protection of Civil Rights Act, 1955

Based on the recommendation of the Committee, this Act was comprehensively amended in 1976 and its name was changed to "The Protection of Civil Rights Act, 1955". The amended Act came into force from 19th November 1976. Report on Prevention of Atrocities against SCs and STs and for matters connected therewith, was made cognizable and non-compoundable offence and the terms of improvement were enhanced. The State Governments have been empowered to impose collective fines on the inhabitants of any area found committing and abetting the commission of untouchability offences. This Act, along with the Rules framed there under, lays down elaborate procedure for ensuring protection of the victims of such practices by providing for special courts, special prosecution, fixing period for investigation, etc.

Preventing Control over Fruits Of Labour
Bonded Labour System (Abolition), Act 1976

Bonded Labour system refers to work in slave like conditions in order to repay a dept for survival and meeting certain urgent and basic necessities of life for which they are charged exorbitant interest. Due to their illiteracy, lack of bargaining power and extremely low wages, creditors manage to create a situation where the dept is never liquidated and consequently the debtor has to render labour in lieu thereof.

The Bonded Labour System (Abolition) Act, 1976 abolished all agreements and obligations, including customary sanctions which permit bonded labour system in various forms. The Act also released all such labourers from these obligations, cancelled their outstanding debts and prohibited creation of any new bodage agreement. The Act also mandatorily provided for economic rehabilitation of freed bonded labour by the State. Keeping a bonded labour is a violation of law and is punishable with sentence of 3 years imprisonment and a fine of Rs. 2,000/- Ministry of Labour operates a centrally sponsored scheme for rehabilitation of released bonded labours.

The Minimum Wages Act, 1948

This Act provides for fixing of minimum rates of wages in different employments and appointment of Committees or Subcommittees for this purpose. The Act also fixes the norms of hours of work, rest and overtime rates. The machinery for enforcement of the Act has also been provided.

Equal Remuneration Act, 1976

The Act mandates that there shall be no discrimination in the payment of wages to women workers performing same or similar nature of work as men.

Child Labour (Prohibition and Regulation) Act, 1986

The Act prohibits the engagement of children in certain employments and regulates the conditions of work of children in certain others. It outlines severe penalties for those violating its provisions. The Act also provides for a Child Labour Technical Advisory Committee to advise the Central Government on which occupations and industrial processes the employment of child labour should be prohibited.

Various other laws which prohibit the employment of child labour on grounds of safety, etc. include The Children (Pledging of Labour) Act, 1933, The Employment of Children Act, 1938, Factories Act, 1948, Plantation Labour Act, 1951, The Mines Act, 1952, The Merchant Shipping Act, 1958, The Motor Transport Workers Act, 1961, The Bidi Cigar Workers (Conditions of Employment) Act, 1966, The Shops and Commercial Establishment Acts, etc.

Curbing Unequal Distribution of Economic Assets
Land Reforms Laws

The Agrarian structure in the country prior to independence was characterized by high degree of concentration of land by a small section of society and the actual cultivators of land were acutely exploited by them. Land Reforms Policy, introduced in the country after independence, introduced a fivefold programme to check this concentration of economicpower. The policy abolished intermediaries from ownership of land and conferred this right on the tillers of the soil should be its owner. A radical redistribution programme of land among the landless agricultural labour was undertaken by introducing ceiling on land holding and acquisition of surplus land for this purpose.

Through the programme of consolidation of land holdings, arrangements were made under which small parcels of land could be exchanged for a compact contiguous plot through mutual adjustment in the village. Land records were also sought to be updated so that rights and interests of cultivators were safeguarded against manipulation. Land reforms laws were enacted and other regulatory arrangements were made giving effect to this policy by all States.

Debt Relief Legislations

Indebtedness is a chronic problem of all poor persons but it affects SCs/STs more severely. Indebtedness arises because of their poverty and therefore need to borrow for subsistence and to meet other emergent social expenditure like illness, marriage, etc. 18 Report on Prevention of Atrocities against SCs & STs since no such credit is available from institutional sources, money is borrowed from private money lenders who charge exorbitant rates of interest. Due to their inability to pay back, the borrowers are enmeshed in a vicious cycle of debt-bondage.

National Human Rights Commission

The Human Rights Act, 1993 seeks to provide regulatory framework for protection of rights related to life, liberty, and quality, dignity of individuals guaranteed by the constitution or embodied in the International Covenants and enforceable by courts in India. Section 3 of the Act provides for constitution of National Human Rights Commission and section 21 provides for constitution of State Human Rights Commission. In pursuance of section 3, a National Human Rights Commission is already in existence since 12th October, 1993. It takes up the cases regarding human rights violations addressed to it and through its own initiative. As atrocities on SCs are violation of Human Rights, it intervenes in complaints relating to them also. The Commission is also required to submit a report annually which is laid on the table of both Houses of Parliament.

National Commission for Women

Section 3 of National Commission for Women Act, 1990 provides for the constitution of National Commission for Women to investigate and examine all matters relating to safeguards provided for the women under the Constitution and various other laws. The First National Commission was constituted on 31st January, 1992. It takes up Social Justice. The Legal Instruments complaints of women referred to it for redressal irrespective of caste. Accordingly, problems of SC women including those of physical violence against them are also dealt with by it. As other statutory Commissions, the commission has to submit a report annually which is laid on the table of both the Houses.

Effects of Globalization Policy on Welfare State

The problem faced by the weaker section is further compounded by the adoption of the new economic policy with emphasis on globalization. The main features of globalization policy which have adverse implications to these sections are the following:

Being a market-friendly policy, globalization envisages retreat of State from the life of people. Retreat of State has occurred in two areas: first, there is downsizing of the Government resulting in loss of opportunities in the Government sector. This measure affects the weaker sections more than others, because exactly when the State as a means of ensuring justice has provided job quotas to the weaker sections, jobs in Government have begun to shrink. As the space vacated by the State is expected to be filled by the private sector, the latter will expand and touch each and every aspect of the life of people. Thus, with a view to reducing the fiscal deficit, when the government has cut down spending, sectors like health and education seemed to have suffered more. This affects the weaker sections more than others because at a time when these sections have realized the importance of human resource development and when they have made a beginning to use education and health facilities the gradual withdrawal of State from these sectors comes as a bolt from the blue. It is true that private capital is entering into the education and health sectors to fill the vacuum created by the retreat of State. Entry of private capital into these sectors, no doubt will improve the quality of services provided. But the problem to be noted is that the weaker sections cannot have access to these services as these services are very expensive.

On the social front too, we have made significant gains. Removal of untouchability and treating everybody as equal before the law were nothing less than silent, yet profound revolutions. But, unfortunately, we have not been successful in ensuring that the fruits of development reached the lower-most strata of society. Poverty, illiteracy, high rates of infant and maternal mortality, adverse gender ratio, unemployment, poor health-care system, caste, gender and religion-based prejudices and incidences of farmers. suicides are issues that have remained as blots on our democracy. It is still a matter of great distress that we have not been able to ensure a decent living condition for our large working class.

Our economy grew at an average annual rate of about 7 per-cent, about 40 per cent of the world.s poor still live in India and at the same time the number of billionaires is growing. In spite of the completion of ten Five Year Plans and implementation of numerous developmental schemes, nearly one third of our population is living below the poverty line. More than a fifth of our population still does not have any access to quality of health-care. With about a third of our population being illiterate, we are home to the largest number of illiterates in the world. A country with such an unequal distribution of opportunities and wealth can hardly promise long-term security and stability.

Yet another serious problem before us concerns the justice delivery system that we have in place in our country. The legal system in India has sound institutional foundations incorporating all basic democratic principles of impartiality, secularism and equality before law. But, as we can see, in practice the functioning of our justice delivery system is at variance with certain democratic ideals because of some organs of our Constitution are trying to encroach into others domain and thereby creation distortions.

Conclusion

The position of weaker sections is said be vulnerable. The ancient period people from Panchama varna were not been treated as human being. They had to stay in the outs-cuts of villages. No specialties have been extended to them. After emergence of British Christians missionaries have changed their position to some-extent. The efforts of Jhotibha Phule and Ambedkar are met with partial success. The enforcement of Constitution of India has brought remarkable change in the lives of weaker sections. Part III and Part IV haveprovided social equality, economic equality political justice for development of these people. Reservation policy though not successful completely, but is helpful to same extent for development of weaker sections. The atrocities committed against weaker section are being dealt with by SC and ST Commission, which has been existed with legal powers. Similarly, the atrocities committed on women including the women from weaker sections being monitor by National Commission for women. The labour sections also protect by various legislations, but after introduction of the globalization the implementation of labour laws are liberalized. All these efforts are meager for upbringing weaker sections. Having awareness would be the main criteria for maintain equality in societies.

"Nonetheless, we all agree that mere enactment of laws does not guarantee the eradication of the related problems. Proper implementation of the legislations is necessary to ensure that the intended beneficiaries get the optimum benefits. Further, to tackle the problems in a holistic manner, it is imperative to think and go beyond the legislative initiatives." –Blurb

References
1. Baruah, Aparajita. (2007). Preamble of the Constitution of India: An Insight & Comparison. Eastern Book Co., Ahmadabad.
2. Basu, Durga Das. (2008). Introduction to the

Constitution of India South Asia Books.

3. Das, Hari Hara. (2002). Political System of India. Anmol Publications, New Delhi.

4. Jayapalan, N. (1998). Constitutional History of India. Atlantic Publishers & Distributors, New Delhi.

5. Khanna, Hans Raj. (1981). Making of India's Constitution. Eastern Book Co., Ahmadabad.

6. Pylee, M.V. (2004). Constitutional Government in India. S. Chand & Co., Bombay.

7. Sen, Sarbani. (2007). The Constitution of India: Popular Sovereignty and Democratic Transformations. Oxford University Press., New Delhi.

8. Sharma, Dinesh; Singh, Jaya; Maganathan, R.; et al. (2002). Indian Constitution at Work. Political Science, Class XI. NCERT., New Delhi.

9. "The Constituent Assembly Debates (Proceedings): (9th December, 1946 to 24 January 1950)". The Parliament of India Archive.

10. Reddy G B. (2009). Constitution of India and Professional Ethics, I.K. International Publishing House Pvt. Ltd., New Delhi.

11. Reddy., G.B. (2009). Land Laws in A.P., Gogia Law Agency, Hyderabad.

12. Misra.S.N. (2009). Labour and Indutrial laws, Gogia Law Agency, Hyderabad.

13.http://parliamentofindia.nic.in/ls/debates/debates.htm

14. www.hrcr.org

15. www.idsn.org

16. www.ambedkar.org

17. www.mcrg.ac.in

18. http://practiceiparticipation.org Abhinav International Monthly Refereed Journal of Research In Management & Technology 129

ISSN – 2320-0073 Volume II, September'13

www.abhinavjournal.com

19. www.hindustantimes.com

20. http://planningcommission.nic.in

21. www.unhchr.ch

22. http://indiankanoon.org

23. www.slideshare.net

24. www.researchgate.net

25. www.academia.edu
26. www.lawteacher.net
27. www.right-to-education.org
28. www.un.int
29. www.articlesbase.com
30. http://labour.nic.in
31. www.tehelka.com
32. http://wcd.nic.in
33. www.indianetzone.com
34. http://tribal.nic.in
35. www.legistationonline.org

GOVERNING THE RURAL ECONOMY OF INDIA: THE MECHANISM OF PANCHAYATI RAJ INSTITUTION

Ms. Darshana S. Rohit[1],   Dr. Sangita Prajapati[2]

[1] *Assistant Professor, Post Graduate Department of Business Studies, Sardar Patel University, Vallabh Vidyanagar*

[2] *Project Fellow (UGC-SAP-DRS-II) & Faculty in CAB, Post Graduate Department of Business Studies, Sardar Patel University, Vallabh Vidyanagar*

Abstract

The best, quickest and most efficient way is to build up from the bottom, every village has to become a self-sufficient republic. This does not require brave resolutions. It requires brave, corporate, intelligent work-Mahatma Gandhi. Panchayat system is a unique creation of Indian political system. In the literal sense it means the assembly of five most proficient, wise and revered elders selected by the village community. Well, this is in no way a recent phenomenon and has been prevalent in the rural India from ancient days. In general the responsibility conferred upon them is to settle all kinds of disputes between individuals and villages by the means of mutual settlements. However, in the recent years the Union Government of India has taken lots of measures to empower the village panchayats in a better manner. For greater advancements to this effect the government has decentralized several administrative functions to the village level that have undoubtedly made the panchayats more able. Even though this system is ancient, this administrative system has been recommended by Mahatma Gandhi in the modern age. He in real terms advocated the establishment of Panchayat Raj, which would be the ideal decentralized form of government meant for the development and empowerment of the village. In both content and implementation it would work as the foundation of the Indian political scenario. If the development continues it would lead to self-governance in the subsequent periods. Panchayats in India are an age old institution for governance at village level. In 1992, through the enactment of the 73rd Constitutional Amendment, Panchayati Raj Institutions (PRI) was strengthened as local government organizations with clear areas of jurisdiction, adequate power, authority and funds commensurate with responsibilities. This paper is an attempt to present some of the important highlights of Panchayat system in India, It covers the history, ideas, objectives, the present scenario, the structure, powers, responsibilities, duties, functioning, the administrative set-ups, various sources of revenue of the panchyats in India and lastly the concluding remarks.

Introduction

For sustainable economic and social development to take place in any country, it is necessary that people participate in the political process. The process of participation is complex- and it is by no means clear that it is comprehensively inclusive. It is not possible to assume that all sections of the population take part effectively in the political and democratic processes of society. There are many reasons why people may not participate: from apathy to a sense of helplessness.

The institutional framework of local government was introduced by British rule, but at that time it was far away from the self-government as well as from its role of independence. This division of power including panchayat level was introduced from above without any connection of institutions and existing social order and communities. The Indian population was integrated to the panchayat idea only bureautically. The people were considered as the subject, but the process of modernization of local government began even during the British domination period, implied the vision to provide to the people the status of citizenship. Thus the rural self-government presented an institutional tool to accomplish such transformation through the process of transferring sovereignty, autonomy and representative character to the panchayats. Especially panchayat institutions have the main responsibility to develop any relationship between electorate on the present view and bureaucratic machinery of the state.

A Panchayat is a local government in India. Panchayats are headed by a Sarpanch who is elected by the council. The word Panchayat literally means governance by a council of five when translated into English. They are divided up to districts comprising anywhere between 200 and 600 villages. The Panchayat is often associated with a grass roots style of democracy as even people from the lowest part of the economic spectrum still have a say in who represents them.The institution of Panchayati Raj is specifically designed for the rural population with the basic objective of democratic decentralization and devolution of power with a view to ensuring rapid socio-economic progress with every individual being the architect of his/her own government.

The panchayat raj is a South Asian political system mainly in India, Pakistan, andNepal. "Panchayat" literally means assembly (ayat) of five (panch) wise and respected elders chosen and accepted by the local community. Traditionally, these assemblies settled disputes between individuals and villages. Modern Indian government has decentralized several administrative functions to the local level, empowering elected gram panchayats. Gram panchayats are not to be confused with the unelected khappanchayats (or caste panchayats) found in some parts of India.

The History, Ideas and Objectives of Panchayati Raj in India

During the time of the Rig-Veda (1200 BC), evidences suggest that self-governing village bodies called 'sabhas' existed. With the passage of time, these bodies became panchayats (council of five persons). Panchayats were functional institutions of grassroots governance in almost every village. The Village Panchayat or elected council had large powers, both executive and judicial. Land was distributed by this panchayat which also collected taxes out of the produce and paid the government's share on behalf of the village. Above a number of these village councils there was a larger panchayat or council to supervise and interfere if necessary. Casteism and feudalistic system of governance under Mughal rule in the medieval period slowly eroded the self-government in villages. A new class of feudal chiefs and revenue collectors (zamindars) emerged between the ruler and the people. And, so began the stagnation and decline of self-government in villages.

During the British rule, the autonomy of panchayats gradually declined with the establishment of local civil and criminal courts, revenue and police organisations, the increase in communications, the growth of individualism and the operation of the individual Ryotwari '(landholder-wise) system as against the Mahalwari or village tenure system.

Panchayats in India are an age old institution for governance at village level. In 1992, through the enactment of the 73rd Constitutional Amendment, Panchayati Raj Institutions (PRI) was strengthened as local government organizations with clear areas of jurisdiction, adequate power, authority and funds commensurate with responsibilities. Panchayati Raj is a system of governance in which gram panchayats are the basic units of administration. It has 3 levels: village, block and district.

The term 'panchayat raj' is relatively new, having originated during the British administration. 'Raj' literally means governance or government. Mahatma Gandhi advocated Panchayati Raj, a decentralized form of Government where each village is responsible for its own affairs, as the foundation of India's political system. This term for such a vision was "Gram Swaraj" (Village Self-governance).

It was adopted by state governments during the 1950s and 60s as laws were passed to establish Panchayats in various states. It also found backing in the Indian Constitution, with the 73rd amendment in 1992 to accommodate the idea. The Amendment Act of 1992 contains provision for devolution of powers and responsibilities to the panchayats to both for preparation of plans for economic development and social justice and for implementation in relation to twenty-nine subjects listed in the eleventh schedule of the constitution

Panchayat Raj (Rule of Village Committee) system is a three-tier system in the state with elected bodies at the Village, Taluk and District levels. It ensures greater participation of people and more effective implementation of rural development programmes. There will be a Grama Panchayat for a village or group of villages, a Taluk level and the Zilla Panchayat at the district level.

India has a chequered history of panchayati raj starting from a self-sufficient and self-governing village communities that survived the rise and fall of empires in the past to the modern legalized institutions of governance at the third tier provided with Constitutional support.

Generally the establishment of panchayat election is seen as a step towards decentralization of the central power, decision making and ensuring democracy downward to the villages. The very first idea of the self governance came from the Mahatma Gandhi's vision of "Gram Swaraj" meant primarily the self-rule of the village community and reduction of the power for the central government and provinces. The transference of power flew in his vision from bottom to top, meant from village communities to districts, provinces and finally to the centre. This image was one of the elements of his individual freedom and democracy concept. Gandhi's conceptualization of powers for communities had practical consequence in incorporation some of his principles into the Article 40 of the Constitution, which requires the state government to constitute Gram Panchayat. Gandhi's idea of self-rule of the village community actually emanated from his premise that the real democracy must be direct these ideas were crucial in the times of constitution making process, but seemed to be unpractical or even as anarchistic.

On the contrary Jawaharlal Nehru (prime minister from 1947 to1961) considered panchayat governance as the governance through the self-governing institutions and seemed to him as manipulative from its nature. In his logic this type of governance had only practical vindication in the sense of legitimization of the developmental projects in the particular localities of the country. Meaning that Nehru had no concern to replace or modernize the bureaucratic administration at the bottom level in the institutional framework, even for development purpose of the whole country.

The institutional extension was after all gradually shaped by Rajiv Gandhi (prime minister 1984-1989) visions, which were mainly formed in the context of panchayat, to connect the practice of democracy with the bureaucracy through the so called "power brokers", which was the metaphor for the MP's. These MP's in Rajiv's vision were mediators with their first concern to reach the states benefits for the local citizens. This idea was not crucial for the development of local government institutions. The real step towards representative system and democratic governance at the district level was the giving to the panchayat raj a constitutional status. The practical outcome of such venture was reflected in the future 73th and 74th constitutional amendment. They were mainly initiated by Rajiv Gandhi during his prime minister era.

In general, his government declared three tier-pachayati raj institutions, implying their specified rights. 73th amendment envisages devolution process. Rajiv Gandhi was known for the advocacy of local democracy, but he was not the only one who was confident to the local democracy in India. In advance of his governing also political situation between 1970´s and 1980´s he contributed to the idea and implementation of decentralization process.

Panchayats presented decentralization of the state on the basis of self rule and administrative control over the village society and economy. Not only that. Panchayat elections represent powerful instrument of bridging the rural areas with government. Especially in the 80´s when one of the powerful incentives of Janata government was to maintain panchayat elections in an effort to consolidate the rural power by mobilization of rural electorate, which after all we are observing in contemporary federal elections. Panchayats also represented a precondition of rural development and rural reforms which were connected in the sense of decision making and financial support to the central state power through the Union Ministry of Rural Development.

Present Scenario

At present, there are about 3 million elected representatives at all levels of the panchayat one-third of which are women. These members represent more than 2.4 lakh Gram Panchayats, about 6,000 intermediate level tiers and more than 500 district panchayats . Spread over the length and breadth of the country, the new panchayats cover about 96 per cent of India's more than 5.8 lakh villages and nearly 99.6 per cent of rural population. This is the largest experiment in decentralization of governance in the history of humanity. The Constitution visualizes panchayats as institutions of self-governance. However, giving due consideration to the federal structure of our polity, most of the financial powers and authorities to be endowed on panchayats have been left at the discretion of concerned state legislatures. Consequently, the powers and functions vested in PRIs vary from state to state. These provisions combine representative and direct democracy into a synergy and are expected to result in an extension and deepening of democracy in India. Hence, panchayats have journeyed from an institution within the culture of India to attain constitutional status.

Panchayat and Panchayati Raj System: Structure

The Panchayat system in India follows a three-tier structure: **(i) The Village Panchayat or Gram Panchayat: It operates at the village level. (ii) Panchayat Samiti:** It is the primary executive body and performs its functions at the Block level. **(iii) Zila Parishad**: It operates at the districts level. Zila Parishad executes and coordinates programs of rural development ensures the direct participation of people at the grass root level.

Panchayati Raj Institutions – the grass-roots units of self-government have been proclaimed as the vehicles of socio-economic transformation in rural India. Effective and meaningful functioning of these bodies would depend on active involvement, contribution and participation of its citizens both male and female. The aim of every village being a republic and Panchayats having powers has been translated into reality with the introduction of the three-tier Panchayati Raj system to enlist people's participation in rural reconstruction.

Nodal Agency

In the State level, Panchayats & Rural Development Department of the Government of West Bengal is the Nodal Agency for Implementation, Supervision & Monitoring of the major poverty alleviation programmes in the rural areas of this State and at the District-level, Zilla Parishad is the implementing agency for the same.

Under three-tier system of democratic decentralization, Zilla Parishad is the apex body at the district level followed by Panchayat Samitis at Block level as second-tier and Gram Panchayats, the third-tier.

Zilla Parishad

The Zilla Parishad, Hooghly is functioning at its own office building "Zilla Parishad Prasasanik Bhavan" at the district head-quarter Chinsurah after constitution of Zilla Parishad. The Parishad consisting of 47 members of Zilla Parishad constitution. These total 47 members include Sabhadhipati, Sahakari-Sabhadhipati & 9 Karmadhakshyas.

This Zilla Parishad has constituted 10 nos. of standing committees i.e. Sthayee Samities. Chairman of the standing committee have been elected by and from among the elected members of Parishad for reviewing the schemes.

The respective standing committees of the Parishad deals with the matter assigned to them. There is provision for holding 3 – 4 Zilla Parishad meetings in a year. Besides the Savapatis of Panchayat Samities of this district are the Ex-Officio Members of the Hooghly Zilla Parishad. Moreover, all the MPs and MLAs of the district Hooghly are also the Ex-Officio members of the Zilla Parishad as per West Bengal Panchayat Act 1973.

The District Magistrate & Collector is the Executive Officer of Zilla Parishad, ADM(P&RD) is the Additional Executive Officer and then Secretary, Deputy Secretary & Additional Deputy Secretary are the other officers of the Administration of the Zilla Parishad.
The Executive Officer is the administrative head of the Zilla Parishad and Secretary is the drawing & disbursing officer of the Zilla Parishad.

The Organizational Structure is given in the diagram below.

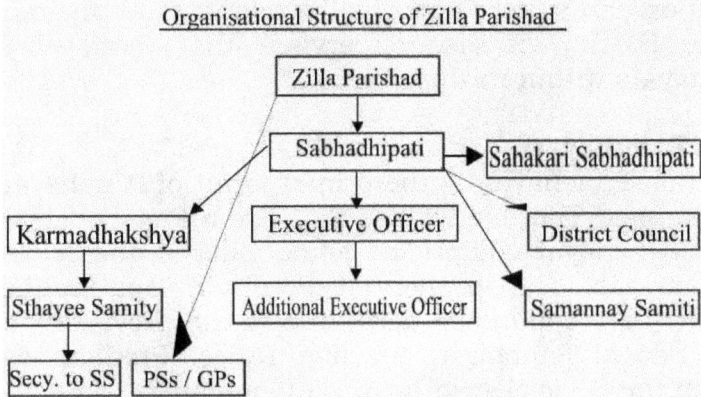

Organisational Structure of Zilla Parishad

Responsibility

The various Rural Development Works carried at the Villages, Gram Panchayats, Block and District levels are planned, implemented, monitored and maintained by the Zilla Parishad. These works are monitored on the State Level by the Panchayats & Rural Development Department of the Government of West Bengal and on the National level by the Govt. of India. The Z.P. at the district level is responsible for the development and welfare works carried through the central, state share and its own funding. Zilla Parishad supervises the works of Panchayat Samities as well as Gram Panchayats within its Jurisdiction.

Panchayat Samities

There are 18 Panchayat Samities in the district. Each Panchayat Samiti is functioning with the Community Development at the Block level created by the government in the Panchayats & Rural Development Deptt. Each Panchayat Samiti consists of official and elected members. The official members are the Block Dev. Officer and the Officers of various State Govt. Deptt. ordinarily stationed at the Block level. The official bearers include the Panchayat Samiti members and the Pradhan of the Gram Panchayats. Savapati is the head of the body and is elected directly by the Panchayat Samiti members. And BDO of the respective block is the Executive Officer of the Panchayat Samity The main functions of the Panchayat Samitis are planning, execution and supervision of all developmental programmes in the Block . It also supervises the works of Gram Panchayats within its Jurisdiction.

Gram Panchayats

Gram Panchayat is the primary unit of Panchayati Raj Institutions. The district has 210 Gram Panchayats. Each Gram Panchayat comprising some villages and is divided into mouzas. The election of Pradhan, Upa-Pradhan & members are conducted according to the provisions of the West Bengal Panchayat Election Rules. Pradhan as the head of the GP is elected by the G.P. members.

Gram Sabha

The Gram Sabha is the most powerful foundation of decentralized governance by ensuring elected representatives are directly and regularly accountable to the people. The aim of the government has been to strengthen the Gram Sabha by introducing favorable policy changes. However, the Gram Sabhas are yet to become operational entities and to do justice to their potential for making the Panchayat system truly self-governed and a bottom-up structure.

Some of the key features in relation to Gram Sabhas are as follows

- The quorum for a Gram Sabha meeting remains one tenth & it is essent ial to have one-third of the quorum as women members.
- The Gram Sabha will work as a supervisory body, and audit and regulate the functioning of Gram Panchayats.
- Recommendations of the Gram Sabha will be binding on the Gram Panchayat.
- The Gram Sabha can approve as well as audit expenditure up to three lakhs.
- The Panchayat Karmi (Panchayat Secretary appointed by the Panchayats but drawing salary from the state government) can be removed from his/her post only if the Gram Sabha approves it.
- All the villages within a Gram Panchayat can have separate Gram Sabhas.
- The Gram Sabha will have the right to recall the Pradhan after two and a half years of commencement of his/her tenure.

The key roles entrusted to the Gram Sabha are microplanning, social audit of Panchayat functioning, ratification of Panchayat accounts, balance sheets, identification and approval of beneficiaries, and supervisory and regulatory functions. **The following indicators were chosen for assessing the prevailing situation in the field:**

- Participation and level of awareness of the Gram Sabha.
- Issues of discussion and the process of decision-making.
- Pattern of leadership.

- Capacity of Gram Sabhas.
- Transparency and accountability of the three tiers (GP, PS & ZP) to the Gram Sabha.

Administrative Setup

State-wise Number of Panchayats in India (1991)	
States/UTs	No. of Panchayats
Andhra Pradesh	19517
Arunachal Pradesh	860
Assam	2162
Bihar	11653
Goa	183
Gujarat	13311
Haryana	5790
Himachal Pradesh	2597
Jammu & Kashmir	1469
Karnataka	2536
Kerala	983
Madhya Pradesh	18801
Maharashtra	25595
Manipur	166
Meghalaya	-
Mizoram	622
Nagaland	980
Orissa	4395
Punjab	10953
Rajasthan	7363
Sikkim	138
Tamil Nadu	13261
Tripura	911
Uttar Pradesh	73927
West Bengal	3305
Andaman & Nicobar Islands	44
Chandigarh	21
Dadra & Nagar Haveli	10
Daman & Diu	10
Delhi	191
Lakshadweep	-
Pondicherry	-
India	221754

Responsibilities of the Gram Panchayats

(1) The Gram Panchayat shall be responsible for identification of the projects in the Gram Panchayat area to be taken up under a Scheme as per the recommendations of the Gram Sabha and the Ward Sabhas and for executing and supervising such works.

(2) A Gram Panchayat may take up any project under a Scheme within the area of the Gram Panchayat as may be sanctioned by the Programme Officer.

(3) Every Gram Panchayat shall, after considering the recommendations of the Gram Sabha and the Ward Sabhas, prepare a development plan and maintain a shelf of possible works to be taken up under the Scheme as and when demand for work arises.

(4) The Gram Panchayat shall forward its proposals for the development projects including the order of priority between different works to the Programme Officer for scrutiny and preliminary approval prior to the commencement of the year in which it is proposed to be executed.

(5) The Programme Officer shall allot at least fifty per cent, of the works in terms of its cost under a Scheme to be implemented through the Gram Panchayats.

(6) The Programme Officer shall supply each Gram Panchayat with—
(a) the muster rolls for the works sanctioned to be executed by it; and
(b) a list of employment opportunities available elsewhere to the residents of the Gram Panchayat.

(7) The Gram Panchayat shall allocate employment opportunities among the applicants and ask them to report for work.

(8) The works taken up by a Gram Panchayat under a Scheme shall meet the required technical standards and measurements.

119

State Wise Responsibilities of Panchayat

State	Level of Panchayat	Responsibilities Of Their Panchayat
All most all the states	Village level	1. preparation of annual plans 2. preparation of annual budget 3. mobilizing relief for natural calamities 4. removal of encroachment on public properties 5. organizing voluntary labour and contribution for community works 6. maintenance of statistics of villages 7. functions entrusted by Panchayat Samiti, Zilla Panchayat, State or Central government
	Block level	1. general administrative functions 2. developmental and social functions 3. maintenance functions
Many states	Village and block level	Developmental activities include: Agriculture social forestry, animal husbandry, drinking water, rural housing, education, social welfare, small scale industries
Andhra Pradesh, Maharashtra, West Bengal	Village level	General administrative functionsVillage defence, information and Publicity Constitution of Nyaya Panchayats
Himachal Pradesh, Madhya Pradesh, Rajasthan	Village level	Regulation of liquor shops
Gujrat, Himachal Pradesh, Maharashtra	Village level	Regulation and construction of hoses
Andhra Pradesh, Gujrat, Madhya Pradesh and West Bengal	Village level	Protection and repair of buildings and properties

Andhra Pradesh	Village level	Construction of jhuggies
Andhra Pradesh, Gujrat, Maharashtra, West Bengal	Village level	Destruction of stray animals
Gujrat	Block level	Social education, village defence corps, defence
Gujrat and Maharashtra	Block level	Publicity and information
Gujrat, Maharashtra, and Rajasthan	Block level	Statistics
Karnatka, Maharashtra, Rajasthan	Block level	Social reform
Gujrat and West Bengal	Block level	Rural credit
Gujrat, West Bengal, Maharashtra	District level	Technical advisory role
Gujrat and West Bengal	District level	Relief measures
Maharashtra	District level	Publicity
Gujrat	District level	Development of village sites
West Bengal	District level	Rural credit
Maharashtra	District level	Maintenance of dharamshalas public functions propagation of gramdan and bhoodan

Powers, Duties, Functions and Administration of Gram Panchayats

Functions of Gram Panchayat – Subject to such conditions as may be specified by the State Government, from time to time, a Gram Panchayat shall perform the following functions, namely –

I- Agriculture including agricultural extension –
➢ Promotion and development of agriculture and horticulture,

121

> Development of wastelands and grazing lands and preventing their unauthorized alienation and use.

II- Land and development, land reform implementation, land consolidation and soil conservation;
> Assisting the Government and other agencies in land development, land reform and soil conservation.
> Assisting in land consolidation.

III Minor irrigation, water management and watershed development;
> Managing and assisting in water distribution from minor
> irrigation projects.
> Construction, repair and maintenance of minor irrigation
> Projects, regulation of supply of water for irrigation purpose.

IV Animal husbandry, dairying and poultry;

> Improving breed of cattle, poultry, and other live stock.
> Promotion of dairying, poultry, piggery etc.

V Fisheries

> Development of fisheries in the villages.

VI Social and farm forestry;

> Planting and preserving trees on the sides of roads and public lands.
> Development and promotion of social and farm, forestry and sericulture.

VII Minor forest produce

> Promotion and development of minor forest produce.

VIII Small industries

What Are the Duties of the Panchayat?
A Panchayat is a local government in India. Panchayats are headed by a Sarpanch who is elected by the council. The word Panchayat literally means governance by a council of five when translated into English. They are divided up to districts comprising anywhere between 200 and 600 villages. The Panchayat is often associated with a grass roots style of democracy as even people from the lowest part of the economic spectrum still have a say in who represents them.

Economic Development
The Panchayat is responsible for determining the amount of tax as well as implementing the collection of such. The Panchayat is also authorized to appropriate the gathered taxes to levy these taxes before giving the state government its due. Another duty is to write grants for state funds based on the respective need of the district they represent. In India, there are three major sources from which Panchayats get their funds. The two major sources are the central government and the State Finance Commission, which gets its money from state governments. Then there are the local bodies that raise money independently of the state or federal governments.

Functioning as an Institution of Self-Government
According to the constitution of India, article 40 states Panchayats should be set up in all villages and act as a self governing institution. The Gram Panchayat is the most basic unit and exists on the village level. The people who sit on this council are drawn from their respective villages. The next level up is the Panchayat Samiti, which is formed by democratically elected members of the Gram Panchayat. At the forefront of the entire system is the Zila Parishdad who draw their ranks from previous members of the Panchayat Samiti.

Social Justice and Its Empowerment
Another duty of the Panchayat is to watch out for injustice and serve for the betterment of the Indian people. Some of the major issues addressed include safe drinking water,

malnutrition, health, corruption and illiteracy. Some of the institutions offered to remedy this include cheap educational options with respect to vocational training and public libraries. For those who can't afford proper health care, subsidized hospitals and counselors who arbitrate disputes are available. Also, water management is funded to insure clean drinking water and to limit water borne illness. This way, the Panchayat is self sustaining with respect to social needs as it theoretically doesn't need any outside help from the federal government.

Sources of income
The main source of income of the panchayat samiti are grants-in-aid and loans from the State Government.

Sources of Income
> Taxes on water, pilgrimage, markets, etc.
> Fixed grant from the State Government in proportion with the land revenue and money for works and schemes assigned to the Parishad.

Revenue
The Village Panchayat is the only body, empowered to levy taxes including fees and charges. The Village Panchayat levies the following taxes:

Tax Revenue
> House tax
> Profession tax
> Advertisement tax

Non-Tax Revenue
> Licensing fee for building plan and
> layout approval
> Fees and charges on D&O trades,
> Market fee,
> Water charges,
> Fee on cart stand
> Social Forestry auctions
> Fishery rentals
> 2-C patta fees
> Income from market and fairs.

> ➤ Fees from ferries
> ➤ 11. Fines and penalties

Avenues for mobilizing more revenue from items such as Mobile towers erected in Panchayat land, OFC laid along Panchayat roads, land categorization, etc., will be explored. A High Level Committee will be constituted by the Government to suggest ways and means to augment resources of the **Panchayats.**

Panchayat Own Revenue Collections

| Sr. No. | State | Per Capita (Rs.) | | | | Ann. Growth Own Rev. 1991-98 (%) |
| | | 1990-91 | | 1997-98 | | |
		GP	All tiers	GP	All tiers	All tiers
1	Haryana	23.68	23.68	37.42	37.46	8.79
2	Meghalaya	15.64	15.64	18.37	18.37	4.91
3	Goa	15.20	15.20	58.32	58.32	20.92
4	Punjab	12.71	15.09	29.75	34.76	13.98
5	Kerala	14.62	14.62	43.27	43.27	17.89
6	Andhra Pradesh	10.74	12.89	21.92	25.92	11.91
7	Gujarat	7.52	10.14	10.45	13.35	5.66
8	Rajasthan	4.93	7.15	3.34	7.64	3.43
9	Maharashtra	6.55	7.07	19.75	21.00	18.49
10	Karnataka	5.58	5.58	8.96	8.96	8.22
11	Tamil Nadu	2.81	4.27	7.27	9.61	11.67
12	West Bengal	1.74	2.88	2.35	3.56	4.67
13	Madhya Pradesh	2.30	2.35	4.71	5.55	15.14
14	Orissa	2.15	2.15	2.33	2.33	2.45
15	Uttar Pradesh	0.30	2.04	0.30	3.61	10.80
16	Assam	1.03	1.51	1.06	1.56	2.01
17	Tripura	0.06	0.06	0.24	0.24	22.95
18	Himachal Pradesh	0.04	0.04	1.29	1.29	65.39
19	Bihar	0.00	0.00	0.00	0.00	0.00
20	Manipur	0.00	0.00	0.00	0.00	0.00
21	Mizoram	0.00	0.00	0.25	0.25	0.00
22	Nagaland	0.00	0.00	0.00	0.00	0.00

23	Sikkim	0.00	0.00	0.00	0.00	0.00
	All	4.23	5.24	8.37	10.17	11.76
	Coeff of var	1.59	1.31	1.95	1.62	

Source: **Rajaraman, 2003, table 2.2.**

Notes:
Figures are for panchayat "own" revenues. GP is Gram Panchayat; all tiers sum the figures for Gram, Taluk and Zilla Panchayats. Per capita figures for 1997-98 are based on estimated rural population for 1997-98, from inter-censal growth rates, merging the three newly created states with parent states. The sum across all states obtained here differs slightly from the all-states aggregate in the Report of the EFC. No revenue data are provided in the report for Arunachal Pradesh and Jammu and Kashmir.

Conclusion
The Panchayats have been entrusted certain responsibilities in the various spheres of primarily developmental activities. After the 73rd Constitution Amenedement Act in 1992 local self-government has official received federal recognition. Local government still remains in the State List and is under the control and competence of Indian state. This practically means that panchayats are financially dependent on the state. So what they receive from the Centre is also linked with what the Centre devolves to the local government. The Panchayats cannot become effective institutions of local self-governance unless they have a strong financial base with clearly defined sources of revenues and the revenues are properly managed to optimize the resources. As per the provisions of the Constitution, the State Legislature has been given the discretion to authorize Panchayats to levy taxes and assign taxes, etc, to enable them to mobilise their own resources for discharging assigned duties and functions. So unless these institutions does not have sufficient autonomy and financial strength, it will be difficult to make them a strong governing body of the rural economy of India.

Reference

ARTICLES:

1. THE EVOLUTION OF PANCHAYATI SYSYTEM IN INDIATHE CAS EON INDIAN STATE-BIHAR: BY VIKTORIA BABICOVA (*POLITICKE VEDY / STUDIES*)

2. REVENUE INCENTIVES AT THE THIRD TIER:BY INDIRA RAJARAMAN

3. RBI CHAIR PROFESSOR, NATIONAL INSTITUTE OF PUBLIC FINANCE AND POLICY, NEW DELHI. THIS PAPER WAS PRESENTED AT A NATIONAL SEMINAR FOR THE TWELFTH FINANCE COMMISSION AT HYDERABAD, 16-17 JANUARY 2004.

4. DECENTRALIZATION OF FINANCE: A STUDY OF PANCHAYAT FINANCES IN INDIA (DRAFT VERSION) BY:NASIR AHMED, CENTRE FOR BUGET AND GOVERNMENT ACCOUNTABILITY (A PROGRAMME OF NCAS, NEW DELHI)

5. RURAL DEVELOPMENT AND PANCHAYAT RAJ DEPARTMENT POLICY NOTE 2011-2012 BY: K.P.MUNUSAMY, MINISTER FOR MUNICIPAL ADMINISTRATION & RURAL DEVELOPMENT

6. MOBILISATION AND MANAGEMENT OF FINANCIAL RESOURCES BY PANCHAYATI RAJ INSTITUTIONS– A STUDY OF HARYANA STATE BY:MAHI PAL\ ASSOCIATE PROFESSOR SPONSORED BY PLANNING COMMISSION GOVT. OF INDIA HARYANA INSTITUTE OF RURAL DEVELOPMENT NILOKHERI-132117 (KARNAL) HARYANA PHONE/FAX : (1745)-246039 PHONE : (1745)-245649, 246044, E-MAIL : HIRDNLK@YAHOO.CO.IN,

7. POLITICS OF INDIA:FROM WIKIPEDIA, THE FREE ENCYCLOPEDIA

8. MANUAL 3: PANCHYAT FINANCE: ROLES AND RESPONSIBILITES

9. CHAPTER IV POWERS, DUTIES, FUNCTIONS AND ADMINISTRATION OF GRAM PANCHAYAT

10. CHAPTER – V FINANCES OF PANCHAYATI RAJ INSTITUTIONS IN MADHYA PRADESH - A MACRO REVIEW

WEBSITES

1. http://en.wikipedia.org/wiki/History_of_panchayati_raj_in_India

2. http://en.wikipedia.org/wiki/Panchayati_raj

3. http:www.Panchayat System in India.htm

4. http:www.panchayat.htm

5. http://www.india.tm/showContent-64/INDIAN PANCHAYATS.html?linkid=64

6. http://infocity.hubpages.com/hub/Panchayat-System-In-INDIA

7. http://www.panchayats.in/php/showContent.php?linkid=81

8. http://www.tamilcanadian.com/page.php?cat=59&id=4899

9. http://www.winentrance.com/general_knowledge/polity/panchayati-raj.html

10. http://www.lawisgreek.com/panchayati-raj-in-india

11. http://priresources.in/OverView/OverViewOfPanchayatiRaj.php

12. http://printfu.org/panchayat+system+in+india

13. http://lawmin.nic.in/ncrwc/finalreport/v1ch8.htm

14. http://iesenvis.nic.in/PAR_of_Panchayats.htm

15. http://www.lawyersclubindia.com/bare_acts/detail s_section.asp?mod_id=15468

16. http://iesenvis.nic.in/PAR_of_Panchayats.htm

MUSLIM GHETTOS IN GUJARAT AFTER 2002 RIOTS: EXPECTATIONS OF MINORITIES FROM SOCIETY & GOVERNMENT

Dr. Damini Shah

Assistant Professor, Social Work Department,
Gujarat Vidyapith, Ahmedabad

Introduction

Ghettoisation affects Muslims economic and educational situation and their relations with other communities. It negates opportunities of social inter-dependence with various communities and strengthens narrow-mindedness. Socio-economic backwardness, deprivation of education, national non-existence and isolation from mainstream developmental process are systemic closely associated with political decisions. Non-implementation and negligence by political leadership, bureaucracy, police and Civil society play very important role here.

An important reason for people to be in ghetto involuntarily is consideration of security. Though they have to live in very bad situation. They face immense difficulties. Density of population, poverty, absence of basic infrastructural facility, small and narrow lanes and by lanes, doors and walls, humiliation from majority community, contempt, discrimination by state, fear, insecurity- these are some of the feeling and circumstance in any ghetto at any time!

Ghetto

Ghetto is a group which is lack of resources and decides together to settle in certain locality. To leave this place is almost impossible for them and they are unable to adjust in other localities. These places are known by the word-Ghetto. Generally, ghettos are integral part urban cities.

According to New World Webster Dictionary (1995) ghettos means any area of urban city where people of minority group have settled.

As per the Random House Dictionary: "It is the area of a city which is densely populated with hutments where especially Negroes or any minority group lives. This happens mostly due to Socio-economic limitations."

Racial segregation and ghettos are intertwined. Voluntary decisions and social limitations give birth to it.

The actual meaning of ghetto here is neglected and rejected population monolith community, island world or Muslim centered habitations. Information regarding Govt. schemes for poor does not reach Muslims because of insensitivity and attitude of Govt. officers in addition to absence of awareness and information. Muslim ghettos are deprived of infrastructural facilities like schools, roads, sewerage and garbage disposal, banks, PH Cs etc. Muslim representation in Panchayats, Assemblies and parliament in less compared to others. In this background, the researcher has visualized them as neglected or rejected community.

Juhapura in Ahmadabad (Non-Voluntary Ghetto)

After each communal riot Muslims started landing here from old city of Ahmedabad. They were mostly from old city and industrial locality. After 1992 and 2002 pogrom middle class Muslims, retired IAS/IPS officers, advocates, professors, doctors, traders etc. came here in searching of security. They migrated from places where they were since generations. The state did not pay attentions to the area as it did to others. It was neglected area. Juhapura area developed since 1985 now overflows with Muslim population. Density in population is increasing after each riot with uni formality of religion.

Thousands of inhabitants of Juhapura imagine this area to be unnatural as there is only one religion presented for them. Living in Juhapur is not a choice but a compulsion as their aspiration is to live in mixed localities. Feeling of insecurity does not leave them which make this area a Muslim ghetto.

Three reasons can be ascribed to the emergence of Juhapura ghetto: (1) Residents have similar religious identity whatever their social, economic or cultural status may be; (2) Juhapura is isolated from the remaining city area not only by the dividing wall but not a single city bus plies here in interior area only private transport runs and (3) this area does not get any developmental benefit which others get at ease and is neglected by the authorizes fully and knowingly.

Prof. Abdul shaban of Tata Institute (EPW Aug 2008 p.72) states that, "Communal riots and divisive politics has created fear psychosis among both the majority and minority communities of the country. After the partition of the nation, Muslims are viewed with suspicion by the divisive organization and are considered as 'the other'.

Communal intolerance and narrow-mindedness strengthen undemocratic tendencies in us and then its worsening effect hardly remains limited to power-politics. It spread to culture, education and tolerance too. Religious separation does not separate us in place of worship only; it separated us even in neighborhood, schools, offices and business-places. Political, social, economic and historical forces have their role in dividing our Hindu-Muslim relationship.

According to the observation of Alex (2004, p.1) responses of this exclusion on political and public affair policies in Europe, India. Israel, South Africa, US and other countries are multifarious. In India, Dalit ghettos are an example of such policies and social stigma and discrimination only.

The intensity of communal carnage in 2002 was so high that not only Muslims ran away in large numbers from old Ahmedabad but many other areas also. After carnage of Gujarat in 2002, there erupted 66 habitation localities in eight districts as per reports of center for social Justice (2007).Out of these, 12 settlements each having more than 50 families in Anand, Sabarkantha and Ahmedabad have been chosen for the study which is the scope or focus of this research. Out of the affected families, 10% respondents in each settlement have been selected. For selections of a sample, certain gap sample selection or quasi-accidental sample selection method has been used by researcher.

Among the respondents in this study, there were 55.3% males and 44.7% females with of 44 years average Males were educated up to secondary and higher secondary level whereas woman were 22% less literate. Average strength of family is six. They were living in their native village/ city since 37 years.

67% had their own houses but were compelled to enter into distress sale. 93% respondent were engaged in such trades where families maintenance was difficult from them. The reported average decrease in monthly income was Rs. 4046 in comparison to their income in villages.

Situation after 2002 riots in Gujarat

They are being pushed to the peripheries of city, away from the mainstream society. Most of the Muslims are self-employed. They work as artisan-workers, small traders, small shop keepers, small hawkers, auto rickshaw drivers and drivers. Information regarding Govt. developmental schemes do not reach up to them because of insensitivity attitude of officers and also absence of awareness. Muslim ghettos are deprived of infrastructural facilities like schools, roads, sewerage and garbage disposal, banks, PHCs etc.

Basic Amenities and Infrastructural Facilities

Compared to other communities Muslim representation in Panchayat Assemblies and Parliaments is much less. Various political parties exploit them as vote banks. Even in the community organization such as Board or Dargah etc. there is absence of democratic participation. Thus they have very limited opportunities in decision-making and natural resources because of limited political awareness and scope of participation.

Opinion, expectation and suggestions of affected Muslim regarding minority ghettos have been presented here which are for Govt. and Society to consider.

Respondents' Opinion on the reasons behind riots:

91% respondents say that those politicians who are in power and those who seek power get it engineered. 25% say that it is because of religious fanaticism. It is a shortcut to achieve political ambitions and is well perceived thus by the minority. They believe that those common man who are dependent on daily wages or earnings do no afford rioting situations.

Benefits of living together by multi religious communities- chart showing opinions of respondents

96% people believe it is advantageous. It will increase their tolerance, feeling of unity, all around development, trades and business, nurture good culture, provide assistance in adverse circumstances etc. They give numerous examples of them. Only 4% does not believe that living together will benefit them. They are much depressed with the situation and yet they very well understand the benefits of multiplicity of Indian culture.

They have faith in 'Unity in diversity' politicians and fanatic religious elements have vested interest and only they disturb the harmony of the society.

Localities based on religion

Showing respondents' opinion 81% of them show its negative effects; such as it may increase misunderstanding among new generation, increase distance between two communities, it may obstruct development of minority and they fear that in future communalism will be more dangerous. Only 19% say religion based living will lessen the problems as there won't be Muslim around Hindus in villages hence no question of quarrels. But they very well understand that such isolated living will do more harm to the minority, will increase distance and misunderstanding, which will ultimately harm the entire society.

Respondents' Opinion on role and expectations of Government

96% express their opinion in saying that Govt. should not show step motherly attitude towards Muslims and their feelings should not be hurt. There should be programs which increase social harmony and fanaticism of any religion need not be condoned.

4% have no hope from the Govt. they have faith in democracy and in constitutional democracy everyone should be treated equally by the Govt. and this is the minimum expectation from Gujarat Govt. it is the duty of the state to see that in democracy and constitutional system, all citizens get equal treatment and social justice. Rajdharma is the responsibility of those sitting on the throne. They tend to forget all these in their vote bank politics.

Respondents' Expectation from society for communal unity

They say that such gatherings should be arranged where two communities mix with each other. Educational facility for Muslims should increase and they should not engage in any fanatical activities. There should be ideological change in majority regarding hatred towards Muslims and they should bury the hatchet and spread the spirit of humanity.

One of the important elements of Gandhiji's constructive programs was to step up Hindu-Muslim amity. Inter religious dialogue can increase tolerance but here in ghettos there is no dialogue and it needs serious thinking how to restart. Civil society must take initiative and Govt. has to sincerely participate as a secular state, then only after a long time the poison may lessen and fanatic elements have no place.

Respondents Suggestion to Governmnt

Riot-affected should get justice and those who are responsible should be punished and Govt. must side with minority for that. Further, the affected should be compensated satisfactorily. Infrastructural facilities should be developed and basic amenities provided. Employment opportunities should be generated and atmosphere should be created wherein, in future religion-based habitations do not emerge due to feeling of insecurity.

If concrete and result- oriented programs are planned and implemented with sincerity then only mutual harmony can increase, prejudices decrease, beliefs change and social cohesion get strengthened: minority's faith and confidence in the impartiality of state is crucially tested in delivery of justice. If the state follows Rajdharma, then only it can prove itself. Govt. must walk extra mile to heal the wounds visible on the life of minority community and for that it must pay attention to the expectations and suggestions of respondents.

Riots, loss due to creation of ghettos, society and Govt. action for communal amity all these need serious consideration and thoughtful opinions and suggestions presented also need sincere thinking. Long term programs should be chalked out to bridge the gap and for atmosphere of mutual harmony.

Action programme and suggestions based on research:

To Government

1) Basic and infrastructural facilities to ghettos in Gujarat for affected, of 2002 riots including schools and dispensaries as per their needs.

2) System for quick and easy access requires compensation to affected persons of 2002 riots. Assist affected people in awarding justice and punishment to those responsible.

3) Extremely poor and needy people should be given BPL cards for benefit of Govt. Schemes.

4) Special schemes of livelihood affected people of 2002 and empowering them with skills of employment and training for economic rehabilitation.Encourage communal harmony efforts by civic society.

5) Police reforms as suggested by the Supreme Court at State and Central level on priority basis. Intensive training workshops for change in approach and attitude of police to be fair, objective and within constitutional limits and shed narrow-mindedness.

6) Exemplary disciplinary action on police officers who did not attend calls during riots or escaped from their assigned duty.

7) Officers of proven integrity and judiciously objective image be posted in communally sensitive districts.

8) Control rooms in communal sensitive areas.

9) Strict action and control over instigating and provocative activity by extremist elements and non-participation or involvement in it by the democratic Govt.

For Social organizations

1) Peace brigades of youth, women and children by leaders of both religions and social workers for inculcating sense of unity and equality and various programmes for it.

2) Documentary films, feature films with message of communal unity and harmony to communities and students of schools and colleges with a view to changing their attitudes.

3) `Group discussions on national, international and regional events with students for developing scientific temperament, analytical ability and perspective, importance of multiplicity of views and flowering of logical and reasoning faculties.

4) Celebration of Memorial Days like Gandhi, Vasant-Rajab martyrdom day among communities.

5) To mitigate sense of isolation among minorities and for information of youth of majority community of such situation, NSS workshops be arranged in such areas.

6) Peace march or workshops by Gujarat Vidyapeeth in such localities so that students have a view of realistic situation of minorities and creation of harmonious atmosphere which will take these values to larger society.

7) For field work, workshops, educational tours, centre residence by students of various universities in this sensitive areas and settlements, active NGOs should be involved.

8) Business groups, professional bodies of both the religions should establish peace brigades where there is neither communal discrimination nor business interests.

9) No emphasis on religion, community, region, caste or race but on Civic Society and

10) Citizenship and work of rehabilitation without any communal or sectarian

Considerations and pressure on Govt. for such programs society and social organizations should support and involve in such activities and programs aiming at social justice.

Indian has multi religiosity, culture and pluralism which is the right way for integration of people and mixed culture. This is interwoven in Indian history. Hindu and Islam religions basic essence has kept the two cultures together and encouraged harmonious efforts.

Monotheism of Islam equality of all human beings and fraternity had much effect on Hindu religion and during Middle Ages it gave birth to bhakti movement in India. Social and religious reformers like Ramanand, Kabir, Nanak etc all contributed in discarding discrimination of castes idol worship and polytheism and made efforts for development of liberty, equality and fraternity. 19th century social & religious reformers, ideology and efforts were much influenced by Islam religion. On the other hand, social life and religion of Muslim had tremendous effect on Hindus with whom they came in contact. Their festivals, rituals, thoughts, beliefs and even religious traditions show Hindu influence. Inter-relationship and its effects on each other is visible on religious and social systems. Not only that, literature, sculpture, music and various arts are also not excluded from the influence of Indian culture.

References

1) (2007). મૂળસોતા ઊખડેલા અસ્તિત્વ અને નકાર વચ્ચે સપડાયેલા:ગુજરાતમાં આંતરિક વિસ્થાપિત થયેલા લોકોની સ્થિતિનો દસ્તાવેજ, ગુજરાત જનસંહાર (2002-2007) સેન્ટર ફોર સોશ્યલ જસ્ટિસ અને અનહદનો રિપોર્ટ .

2) ઉચાટ, ડી.એ. (2009). *શિક્ષણ અને સામાજિક વિજ્ઞાનોમાં સંશોધનનું પદ્ધતિશાસ્ત્ર.* રાજકોટ

3) Alex, Anas. (Aug 2004). "Ethnic Segregation and Ghettos." State Uni. of New York at Buffalo. Retrieved April 12, 2009. Website: https://129.3.20.41/ps/urb/papers/0408/0408006.

4) Christophe, J. and T. Charlotte. (2011). "Facing Ghettoizatoin in Riot City: Old Ahmedabad and Juhapura between Victimisation and Self-help." *Muslims in Indian Cities: Trajectories of Marginalization.* Eds, Laurent Gayer and Christophe Jeffrelot. Noida: Harper Collins. 16-17

5) Shaban, A. (2008). "Ghettoisation, Crime and Punishment in Muslim." *Economic and Political Weekly,* August 16 2008: P. 68-73.

ROLE OF REGIONAL RURAL BANKS IN ECONOMIC UPLIFTMENT OF THE WEAKER SECTIONS IN INDIA

Dr. Dharmendra S. Mistry
Associate Professor
Post Graduate Department of Business Studies
Sardar Patel University,
Vallabh Vidyanagar, Gujarat

Abstract

Regional Rural Banks (RRBs) are often seen as the small man's bank. They have taken deep root and have turn out to be a sort of an indissoluble element of rural credit composition. The potential and the need for diversification of economic activities in the rural areas had begun to recognize and this was a sector where the RRBs could play a meaningful role in the economic upliftment of the weaker sections of the rural society. The present study has been undertaken with an objective to analyze the rural credit to the weaker sections and role played by RRBs in their Economic Upliftment. The study also analyzes their role in the priority and non priority sector landings. It is observed that there is significant difference between outstanding saving deposit and time deposit in RRBs during the study period and therefore null hypothesis is ejected and alternate hypothesis is accepted. It is also from the study that there is significant difference between outstanding advances in priority and non-priority sectors in RRBs during the study period and therefore null hypothesis is ejected and alternate hypothesis is accepted.

Key words: Advances, Deposit, Rural Regional Banks, Weaker sections

Introduction

Regional rural banks (RRBs) were introduced in 26 September 1975 the ordinance was replaced by the Regional Rural Banks Acts, 1976. The RRBs were established with a view to development of agriculture activities in the rural area. They also provide the financial facilities for the development of agriculture trade, commerce and other productive activities to the economically and socially marginalized people in rural India. They also endow with low-cost banking facilities to the poor. They make employment facilities available to the weaker sections by appointing them as the workers of RRBs and thereby raise the standard of living for the socio-economic upliftment of the weaker sections of the rural society.

RRBs are often seen as the small man's bank. They have taken deep root and have turn out to be a sort of an indissoluble element of rural credit composition. They have been playing an important role in rural institutional financing in terms of geographical coverage, customers, out –reach and business volume as contribution to development of the rural economy.

The committee on the financial system 1991 (Narasimham Committee) stressed the poor financial health of the RRBs to the exclusion of every other performance indicator 172 of the 196 RRBs were recorded unprofitable with an aggregate loan recovery performance of 40.8 per cent. The low equity base of a few RRBs, Narasimham committee suggested that the RRBs should be merged with sponsor banks. This proposed readily accepted. The committee suggested that the objective of serving the weaker sections effectively could be achieved only by self-sustaining credit institutions. This step marked a major turning point in the functioning of RRBs. There were also certain organizational problems such as low capital base, multiple ownership lack of trained staff, problem of debt recovery, lock of financial resources etc.

The potential and the need for diversification of economic activities in the rural areas had begun to recognize and this was a sector where the RRBs could play a meaningful role in the economic upliftment of the weaker sections of the rural society. The main aim of the Regional Rural Banks was to meet the excess demand for institutional credit in the role areas, particularly among the economically and socially marginalized sections. RRBs as part of the multi-agency approach to rural credit are eminently suitable to do the job envisaged for them that as district level organizations, they can be trusted to take banking closer to rural household. 90 percent of the RRBs branches opened in these rural areas. The RRBs adopted where before there had no banking facilities. The RRBs adopted new innovations for credit delivery with lower risk of default such as self-help group linked lending , non-priority sector collateralized lending, kisan credit card scheme for landed agriculturists etc.

The present study has been undertaken with an objective to analyze the rural credit to the weaker sections and role played by RRBs in their Economic Upliftment. The study also analyzes their role in the priority and non priority sector landings.

The study is organized as follows: firstly, a brief review of role and contribution of regional rural banks in economic upliftment of weaker section is presented. Section two gives a brief overview over the literature review. Study methodology follows in section three. Result and analysis have been portrayed in section four and final section presents the observations, suggestions and conclusion.

Literature Review
The study by Taimni (1994) highlighted that the fact that not all the cooperative sugar factories in Maharashtra were successful. They suffered from political rivalries, poor management, irrational investment in by-product industries, inadequate finance, and recurrent drought conditions leading to reduced supply of sugarcane.

The study by (Sinh & Vishwa, 1996) found that among the NRM co-operatives, fishermen's co-operatives are perhaps the oldest. It was way back in 1913 that India's first fishermen's co-operative was organised under the name, Karla Machhimar (fishermen) Co-operative Society' in Maharashtra. The state of West Bengal was the next to organise fishermen's co-operatives in 1918. Now India has one National Level Federation, 17 State level federations, 108 Regional/District level federations/ unions, and 12,427 Primary Societies with the total membership estimated at 1.94 million.

The study by Singh & Pundir (2000) found that despite their overwhelming importance in India's rural economy, most of the co-operatives suffer from a variety of internal and external problems. The major constraints identified by the authors include the lack of professionalism in management; an archaic co-operative law, excessive control and interference by government; lack of good elected leadership; small size of business and hence inability to attain financial viability; lack of performance-based reward systems; and internal work culture and environment not congenial to the growth and development of co-operatives as a business enterprise.

The study by Selvamani & Rani (2008) highlighted women participation, problem faced by dairy co-operatives for development of rural women in the globalization environment.

The study by Soundarapandian & Srividya (2008) highlighted milk producers' society is strengthened by increasing the sale time this will also increase the sales to improve the performance of the milk society. Reducing expenses will also increase the profit and reduce the liabilities will improve the financial position of the society.

The study by Ramanujam & Periaswamy (2008) highlighted that dairy co-operatives are more suitable for rural development of developing countries like India.

The study by Jayakumari (2008) highlighted that hygienic quality of raw milk needs to be improved to ensure milk products of higher standards. Payment for milk in India is generally based on its FAT and SNF content. Payments for milk on the basis of microbial loads need to be initiated to enhance quality of milk and make India's milk globally acceptable.

The study by Patil (2008) Found that the operation floods have increased employment, income and consumption of milk of rural people in Maharashtra state.

The study by Ghanekar (2008) highlighted that the agricultural by products provide feed and fodder for the cattle, whereas cattle provide necessary drought power for various agricultural operations. Hence, promoting co-operative dairy sector by providing policy support will definitely be a right strategy to tackle the agrarian crisis.

Study by Veerakumar (2009) identified the problems of milk co-operatives in Kerala, like escalating cost of production, occupational mobility and structural setbacks of the milk co-operatives.

The study by(Dubey et al., (2009) found that Mulkanoor cooperative society is a successful model in the country and there is a need to strengthen the cooperative societies in the country on the same line to meet the demand of food, fodder, shelter and employment for our increasing humen and live-stock population in days to come.

Study by Ramananda (2012) identified which are working more efficient and performance in ratio analysis like Operational Efficiency, Economic Viability and Managerial Competency. In the case of MPCSs of Mysore-Chamarajanagar district milk union, which shows positive impact of all the three measures of ratio analysis. Among the society Thandavapura MPCSs is one of the leading and well performing society in terms of operational efficiency in both measures, economic viability and managerial competency. Taluru milk society earned more profits compared to the other MPCSs in terms of economic viability. But in terms of managerial competency shows Taluru MPCS declined and coming to the 5th place compared to the other MPCS. The Vyshampalyam MPCS occupy first place in terms of managerial competency.

Study by Jayavel (2013) was based on objectives to study the socio-economic conditions and analyse the impact of textile industry on member of weavers of silk co-operative societies in Kancheepuram District. The study found that there are around 60,000 silk weavers, out of them 50,000 weavers work under co-operative fold for more than 80 percent of the weavers co-operatives serve as a social asset in term of giving employment, ensuring a fixed wage implementing Government schemes etc., but at present these weavers face lot of problems related to their occupation.

The study by Selvakumar et al. (2013) was carried out with a view to analyze the income and expenditure; deposits and advances; profitability of RRBs and make inter RRB comparison so that they could make suitable suggestions. They concluded that they should come forward to offer some subsidiary services like marketing assistance, technological assistance, insurance facilities, export facilities to the customers.

The study by Balamuniswamy & Erraiah (2014) found that the objective of serving the weaker sections effectively could be achieved only self sustaining credit institutions. These banks had to become competitive, improve their profitability and conform to prudential regulation of asset classification and provisioning norms on equal grip.

From the above review of observed works, it is clear that different authors have approached role of RRBs in different manner. These different approaches helped in the emergence of more and more literature on the subject over time. It gives an idea on extensive and diverse works on upliftment of weaker sections in India. It has been noticed that the studies of role of RRBs in rural development provide divergent results relating to the study period overlap or coincide. The survey of the existing literature reveals that no specific work has been carried out to examine role and contribution of RRBs in upliftment of weaker sections as well as in the priority and non priority sector landings The present study is an attempt in this direction and therefore, aims to enrich the literature of RRBs and weaker sections.

Methodology and Objectives

Objectives

The Objectives of the study are:
1. To analyze the rural credit to the weaker sections and role played by RRBs in their Economic Upliftment.
2. To analyze their role in the priority and non priority sector landings.

(1) Period of the Study
The study is confined only to a period of five years staring form 2007-08 to 2011-12.

(2) Sample
All RRBs have been taken into account for the study period.

(3) Data
The present study is diagnostic and exploratory use of secondary data. The relevant secondary data have been collected mainly through the data base of RBI, NABARAD and Journal of Indian Institute of Bankers has also referred.

The study takes into account not only saving deposit outstanding but time deposit outstanding also. It also takes into outstanding advances in priority as well as non-priority sector.

Hypotheses of the Study

Following hypotheses have been framed and tested with ANOVA to achieve the objectives of the study:

1. H_0 : There is no significant difference between outstanding saving deposit and time deposit in RRBs.

2. H_1 : There is significant difference between outstanding saving deposit and time deposit in RRBs.

3. H_0 : There is no significant difference between outstanding advances in priority and non-priority sectors.

4. H_1 : There is significant difference between outstanding advances in priority and non-priority sectors.

Result And Analysis

Table 1 Deposit Outstanding Position in RRBs in India (Rs. In Lakhs)

Year	Saving (Rs.)	Time (Rs.)
2007-08	21022	73390
2008-09	24353	89475
2009-10	28710	107104
2010-11	33663	123039
2011-12	37173	135769

Source: Compiled from various issues of statistics of Regional Rural Banks, NABARD, Mumbai,2011-2012

Deposit is the life blood of banking sector. RRBs have various deposit schemes and accept demand (saving) and time (term) deposits. Most popular deposits are saving deposits and term deposits. The saving deposits become popular in India and accounts opened to inculcate and encourage the habit of saving among small income group people. The account holders are paid interest on the

148

minimum balance half-yearly. The number of withdrawals is getting restricted for one time. The deposits accepted for specified periods are called term deposits and are also known as fixed deposits. The account holder agrees do not to withdraw the amount earlier than the specified term. The period stipulated at the time of opening the account itself depending upon when the depositor wants his money back. It helps the banker to deploy the funds for longer period. Accordingly, the fixed deposits provide stable funds and constitute term liabilities of the bank. The rate of interest and other terms and conditions on which the bank accepts these deposits are regulated by Reserve Bank of India under the Banking Regulation Act 1949. Now the fixed deposits are growing in RRBs. The RRBs are generating in the nook and corner of rural India since its inception. They have a local familiarity and mobilized rural savings from the public. The table 1 above reveals that the saving deposits of RRBs have been steadily increasing more than 76 % between 2007-08 and 2011-12; while 85 % increase has been noticed in time deposits during the period.

Table 2 ANOVA of Deposit Outstanding Position in RRBs in India

Source of Variation	SS	df	MS	F
Between Groups	14734542874	1	14734542874	43.85614
Within Groups	2687795720	8	335974465	
Total	17422338594	9		

From table 2, it is revealed that calculated value of 'F' (43.85614) is more than the table value of 'F' (5.317655). Hence, it can be said that there is significant difference between outstanding saving deposit and time deposit in RRBs during the study period and therefore null hypothesis is ejected and alternate hypothesis is accepted.

Table 3 Sector wise Outstanding advances by RRBs in India (Rs. In Lakhs)

Year		
2007-08	58984	10090
2008-09	69030	11502
2009-10	82819	13956
2010-11	100331	17625
2011-12	99000	16300

Source: Compiled from various issues of statistics of Re¬gional Rural Banks, NABARD, Mumbai,2011-2012

It is observed from the table 3 that up to the restructuring of the RRBs, the banks have given top priority to the non-priority sector to get more profits. During the financial sector reforms, the RRBs were able to reach more than 85 per cent of the priority sector outstanding advances. The weaker sections and the unemployed youth have deprived of the loans and advances from the bank for taking up agricultural allied activities and self-employment ventures. Rural artisans and retail trade have become victims. There is one and half and two-fold decrease in the outstanding advances of rural artisans and the retail trade respectively. However, the small scale, village and cottage industries have received a considerable check of loans outstanding (about fifteen fold increase). As a result of the financial sector reforms the loaning operations of RRBs have tended to move towards income / profit fetching sectors like other purposes including home loans, gold loans and loans for real estate. On the other, the recovery of the loans from the term loans that is agricultural allied activities and self-employment programmes is not satisfactory, even in some cases accumulated overdues has increased at borrower level.

Table 4 ANOVA of Sector wise Outstanding advances by RRBs in India

Source of Variation	SS	df	MS	F
Between Groups	11607035748	1	11607035748	68.09876
Within Groups	1363553218	8	170444152.3	
Total	12970588966	9		

From table 4, it is revealed that calculated value of 'F' (43.85614) is more than the table value of 'F' (5.317655). Hence, it can be said that there is significant difference between outstanding advances in priority and non-priority sectors in RRBs during the study period and therefore null hypothesis is ejected and alternate hypothesis is accepted.

Observations, Recommendation and Conclusion

It is observed that there is significant difference between outstanding saving deposit and time deposit in RRBs during the study period and therefore null hypothesis is ejected and alternate hypothesis is accepted. It is also from the study that there is significant difference between outstanding advances in priority and non-priority sectors in RRBs during the study period and therefore null hypothesis is ejected and alternate hypothesis is accepted.

The real growth of Indian economy lies on the emancipation of rural masses from poverty, unemployment and other socio-economic backwardness. Keeping this end in view, Regional rural banks were established by the Government of India to develop the rural economy. The RRBs now looked upon with hope for upgrading the rural India. In the present study, the role of RRBs in the rural credit structure has been deeply analyzed. The objective of serving the weaker sections effectively could be achieved only self sustaining credit institutions. However in the liberalized banking era, these banks had to become competitive, improve their profitability and conform to prudential regulation of asset classification and provisioning norms on equal grip. At last keeping in mind the above views in can be said that the regional rural banks plays on important role in the economic upliftment of the weaker sections of the rural society.

References

1. Balamuniswamy, D., & Erraiah, G. (2014). Role of Regional Rural Banks Finance to Weaker Sections of the Rural Society in India. *Indian Journal of Research* , *3* (1), 206-209.

2. Ghanekar, D. V. (2008). Strengthen Dairy Co-operatives to Tackle Agrarian Crisis. *The Co-operator* , *45* (10), 424-426.

3. Jayakumari, J. J. (2008). Dairy Co-operatives-Crafting India's Economic Development. *Tamilnadu Journal of Co-operation* , *8* (3), 21-23.

4. Jayavel, R. (2013). BLOW OF TEXTILE INDUSTRY ON MEMBER WEAVERS' OF SILK HANDLOOM CO-OPERATIVE SOCIETIES IN KANCHIPURAM DISTRICT. *Asia Pacific Journal of Marketing & Management Review* , *2* (4), 22-29.

5. Patil, S. S. (2008). Co-operative Dairy Movement and Operation Flood in Maharashtra: an Overview. *Southern Economist* , *47* (5), 17-20.

6. Ramananda, M. S. (2012). DAIRY CO-OPERATIVE – VIABLE TOOL FOR RURAL DEVELOPMENT. *International Journal of Research in IT & Management, 2* (11), 10-20.

7. Ramanujam, K. N., & Periaswamy, N. (2008). Development of Dairy Co-operatives. *Indian Co-operative review* , *45* (3), 218-226.

8. Selvakumar, M., Jegatheesan, K., & Aruna, G. (2013). A Performance Evaluation of Regional Rural Banks in India. *The Indian Journal of Commerce* , *66* (1), 84-94.

9. Selvamani, & Rani, C. (2008). Dairy Co-operatives and Development of Rura Women in the Era of Globalisation. *Indian Co-operative review* , *46* (20), 127-135.

10. Singh, K., & Pundir, R. S. (2000). *Co-operatives and Rural Development in India.* Anand: Institute of Rural Management.

11. Sinh, K., & Vishwa, B. (1996). *Co-operative Management of Natural Resources.* New Delhi: Sage Publications.

12. Soundarapandian, M., & Srividya, G. K. (2008). Karukkampalyam Milk Producers Co-operative Society- A Case study. *Indian Co-operative review* , *46* (1), 23-33.

13. Taimni, K. K. (1994). Integrated Co-operatives: The Case of Sugar Co-operatives in Maharashtra. In K. K. Taimni, *Asia's Rural Co-operatives* (pp. 220-245). New Delhi: Oxford & IBH Publishing Co. Pvt. Ltd.

14. Veerakumar, G. (2009). Problems and Prospects of Milk co-operatives in Kerala. *The Co-operator* , *46* (9), 399-402.